Music Marketing [dot] com Presents:

SIX-FIGURE MUSICIAN

How to Sell More Music,

Get More People to Your Shows, and

Make More Money in the Music Business

DAVID HOOPER

Acknowledgements

This book would not have happened without the direction, dedication, and friendship of Wendy Wallace. There is no way I would have completed it without your assistance.

Thanks to the following people for your help over the years: Wendy Burt-Thomas, Bob Baker, Tripp Lanier, Andre Calihanna, Charles Hooper, Kelli Smith, Lawrence Gelburd, Ritch Esra, Stephen Trumbull, Derek Sivers, Norm Kale, Georgia Nix, Mike Levine, Aaron Shepard, Joe Rocha, Laurel Staples, Kim McCollum, Brandi Surface, Jeremiah Nave, Danny Poland, Ernie Petrangelo, Laurel Creech, Gary Kraen, Dan Buckley, Justin Hammel, Lester Turner, Asieren Boyce, Rik Roberts, Micah Solomon, Jenni Leeds, Jim Stamper, Jeff Fellers, Jeff Lysyczyn, and Joe Taylor.

TABLE OF CONTENTS

Read This First   vii

Chapter 1: Make The Commitment   1
Fail Fast, Fail Often • Be a Little Better, Do a Little Better • Which of These 7 Qualities Do You Have? • Is This a Dream? • What Will Happen to the Phone Sex Girls? • Paralyzed Musicians • It Doesn't Have to Be Perfect • The Magic Bullet to Ensure Success In Music

Chapter 2: Choose Your Path   21
Impact • Ease • How to Choose Your Path • Don't Get Too Comfortable • Getting Used to Change • 7 Ways to Get Out of Your Comfort Zone and Start Taking Risks • The Myth of the Overnight Success • Resilience

Chapter 3: Play Your Game   43
The Record Label Fantasy • Payola • Spray and Pray • Musician Wins Lotto • How to Get a Record Deal • Two Different Acts With a Single Thing In Common • Play Your Game • The Do-It-Yourself Record Company Model • Is a Record Deal Right for You? • Don't Wait to Get Started

Chapter 4: Claim Your Space   67
Use a Laser, Not a Wrecking Ball • Your Ideal Customer • Music Marketing Simplified • Fun Works Both Ways • 7 Tips to Build Rapport With Fans (Or Anybody) • "Dance With the One That Brung Ya." • Start Where You Are • The "Secret Code" of Fans • Let Your Freak Flag Fly • Watch for Patterns • Alienate Some People • Embrace the Slow Burn • Flash In the Pan • 9 Ways to Keep Your Career Moving Forward

Chapter 5: Connect With Your Audience   89
Empathy – An Essential (And Profitable) Skill • Two Acts, Two Outcomes • If a Tree Falls and Nobody Is Around to Hear It … • "Those Guys Are Still Around?" • Own the Media • The Power of One • A Word On Fan Relationships • Ways to Engage Fans Using Social Media • 13 Tips for Social Media Success • Social Media Rules for You and Your Team • The Power of Social Media In Offline Integration • Welcome to the V.I.P. Section • One Way to Screw Everything Up and Lose All Your Fans

Chapter 6: Understand Why People Buy Music   117
The Majority of People Are Not Like You • How Most People Think About Music • Know What You're Selling • How to Go Big • The Power of Making People Feel Good • What People Want • This Is Never About You • Your Relationship With Fans • The "Superfan" • Honesty Will Take You a Long Way

Chapter 7: Rise Above The Noise   141

How to Compete (And Win) In the Music Business • Digital Music Is Invisible • The Drip Method • Music Marketing Lessons From a Gas Station • The Value of Music Piracy • If You Can't Beat 'Em, Join 'Em • The Biggest Problem You (And Other Musicians) Will Face • 8 Ways to Make Money Giving Your Music Away for Free

Chapter 8: Find Your Balance   165

What Are Your Music Business Goals? • Are You Moving Closer to Your Goals? • The 80/20 Rule • The Balance of Business and Art • Taking Care of Business • How to Segment Your Work • Your Key to Getting Things Done – a Timer • If You Want Something Done Right … • How to Avoid Burnout

Chapter 9: Be Flexible And Keep Moving Forward   189

The Movie Man • Does This Sound Like You? • Forget the Format and Distribution • Forget the Website • The Harsh Reality of the Music Business (And How to Navigate It)

Final Thoughts   207

Appendix I: It's Your Job To Keep In Touch With Fans (Not The Other Way Around)   211

How to Use Email Effectively • Segment Your Mailing List • Do Email Marketing the Right Way • Give People a Reason to Sign Up for Your List • Sending Postcards • Phone Calls • Audio Messages • Text Messages • Video Messages • Make Fans Feel Important

Appendix II: Music Doesn't Sell Itself – How To Make Money Selling Your Music And Merch   239

The Live Show Experience • The Importance of Social Proof • Best Examples of Selling Music and Merch At Live Shows • Ways to Sell Merchandise At Your Live Show • What to Do When People Say No • Selling Music Beyond the Live Show • Catering to the Collectors • Think Beyond Music

READ THIS FIRST

I started my music marketing company way back in July of 1995. I mention this because you need to know two things:

1. The music business isn't some kind of hobby to me. It's what I do.

   And I do it … Every. Single. Day.

2. The content within this book is the result of almost two decades on the frontline of live, online, and guerrilla music marketing.

This book is not a hastily thrown together "manual" for those looking for quick money in the music business. It has been designed for musicians who want a career in the music business more than they want fame (although some level of fame is often part of the experience).

This is information you can use.

No fluff. No filler.

"Heads I win. Tails you lose."

Have you ever heard that before? I want you to think about this saying as you read this book, because it's what this book is about—setting yourself up to win.

It takes a lot to win.

In the process of winning, you'll often feel like you've lost.

It's painful to book a gig, show up, and have nobody in the audience.

It's painful to record an album, release it, and have it go nowhere.

It's painful when your parents, friends, and even your own spouse don't understand your desire to create music and the sacrifices you're making to be successful in this business.

It's painful, but it's the way things work ... at least for a while. Then you start to get better, more people get into what you're doing, and you get the respect you're seeking.

As tough as it is to win, the cost of giving up and walking away is 1000 times more.

The cost of losing is always wondering what could have been.

The cost of losing is spending your life watching others from the sidelines.

The cost of losing is being stuck at a job you can't stand.

When you think about things this way, you really have no choice but to win.

So what's it going to be?

We both know the answer, don't we?

Let's get going ...

CHAPTER 1:

MAKE THE COMMITMENT

Making the commitment to do what it takes to be successful in the music business consists of two decisions:

- Acknowledging that you, and you alone, are responsible for your music business success, because you are the one making the choice to do something (or not do it).

- Recognizing that every decision you make, even the small ones, is either getting you closer to your music business goals or taking you further away.

You are in control. Sure, there are things happening to both the industry and the world in general that may be out of your hands, but you are the one who is ultimately responsible for whether you succeed or fail.

The wind blows the same direction for everybody. How will you set your sail?

People who complain about problems don't change the world. People who fix problems do.

FAIL FAST, FAIL OFTEN

Most people play things way more safe than they realize.

The only way you'll know how fast you can drive a car is to accelerate until you lose control and crash. Anything less, even if you back off just before losing control, isn't your top speed.

Like a car, the only way you'll know how much you can accomplish in your music career is to reach the point of failure.

If you feel that things in your music business career aren't moving along fast enough, you may want to "crash the car." That's the only way to take things to the maximum level.

Playing balls-out like this is scary, but also extremely motivating. Most of the time, even when you get extremely ambitious with your plans, as long as you've made the decision to "go pro" and have a solid foundation to work from, you won't crash. You'll simply find you're able to work harder, faster, and longer than you once thought.

If you *do* crash, you get up, dust yourself off, and get back on the horse. Then you push forward again, this time, adding what you've learned from your previous experience to hold things steady for a longer period of time.

Each time you go after something using what you've learned from previous experiences, you'll be expanding your capacity to handle the "intensity" of the situation, which means that soon, accomplishing what you want will be easy for you.

Will you always fail? No. A lot of the time, you'll try something new and it will work out great.

If something isn't going to work, you might as well find out now. Don't be the person who sits on an idea for years, only to find out nobody is interested. If no one cares, you want to find out now, so you can either drop the idea or make people care.

Failure is good. It's how you learn what doesn't work. Embrace it.

If you're not failing at anything, you're not putting yourself out there enough or pushing the envelope like you should. Don't play it safe.

BE A LITTLE BETTER, DO A LITTLE BETTER

You don't necessarily have to be a lot better than the next guy. The people making money in this business simply have to be a little better.

Think of a runner in the Olympics. The difference between winning Gold and winning Silver could be less than a second. But the difference in endorsements, recognition, and a long career can be off the charts.

If you want to play, you simply have to be "a little better."

Is the starting quarterback on a football team that much better than the backup? No.

Is the band that gets signed to a record deal that much better than one that doesn't? No.

Is the winner of *American Idol* that much better than the runner-up? No.

It's not hard to understand this concept. The problem is, the older and more successful we get, the more comfortable we get. Why strive for better when "good enough" keeps a roof over your head, food on your plate, and a shirt on your back?

Comfort is the enemy of excellence. This is one of the reasons so many musicians plateau, and even regress, in their careers and talent.

Life should be comfortable though, shouldn't it?

The key to consistent, long-term improvement of yourself is to do it slowly and gradually. Don't think about the time it will take to "get there" or put all your focus on an end goal. Simply make small and consistent improvements, and you'll get wherever "there" is.

> *"Don't let the fear of the time it will take to accomplish something stand in the way of your doing it. The time will pass anyway; we might just as well put that passing time to the best possible use."*
>
> **– Earl Nightingale**

WHICH OF THESE 7 QUALITIES DO YOU HAVE? (You're going to need all of them to succeed in this business ...)

Since 1995, I've worked with (and studied) hundreds of successful musicians. Here are the most important personal characteristics and other aspects they share that have enabled them to do well.

You'll likely already be great at some of these, while others you'll need to cultivate. It's OK to focus on your strengths, but don't neglect what needs work, because everything mentioned here is important, and all are necessary to your music business success.

The Ability to Make the Decision

Let's say you wanted to have a healthier diet. Making the decision is more than, "I'm going to try to eat better." Making the decision is, "I'm going to be vegan."

There is no "middle ground" when you make the decision. There is no "I'll do it if it's convenient." You're either on the path or you're not. I'm talking about actually making the choice to remove "Plan B" from the conversation and going for exactly what you want.

For many musicians, this comes when you quit your day job and 100 percent of your income is derived from music or music-related elements.

When you make the decision to do something, you'll start to act differently. You suddenly have the guts to ask for the money you need, because you know that if you don't, you're not going to have enough food for the week.

Making the decision gets you motivated fast and will increase your hustle. You'll start looking for opportunities to make money with your music, whether it be scoring an independent film, teaching lessons, or playing weddings. It may not always be glamorous, but you'll feel better about yourself, because you know that you're doing it without anything to fall back on.

Knowledge of the Destination

Lewis Carroll said it best:

"Alice and the Cat"

Alice: "Would you tell me, please, which way I ought to go from here?"

The Cat: "That depends a good deal on where you want to get to."

Alice: "I don't much care where."

The Cat: "Then it doesn't much matter which way you go."

Alice: "... so long as I get somewhere."

The Cat: "Oh, you're sure to do that, if only you walk long enough."

Everybody gets "somewhere" eventually. The problem is, if you don't have a specific place in mind, it's usually not any better than where you started. Sometimes it's worse.

Knowing what you want is essential to music business success. It will give you a reference point to work from, so you can adjust your trajectory and avoid wasting needed time and energy on things you have no interest in.

How do you figure out what you want?

- **Dream Big** – Get a blank sheet of paper and write down at least 50 things that you want. Don't censor yourself.

- **Ask Why** – Why do you want these things? You should have a specific answer for everything on your list. If not, it shouldn't be there.

- **Get Focused** – What are your top five goals? This is where you'll start.

Decide where you want to go and make it happen.

Openness and Flexibility

People change and plans change. In addition, as you learn more about what's possible and your capacity to create it expands, new opportunities will become an option. Because of this, avoid getting too stuck on what you want.

As an example, think about the music business and how it has changed over the last several years. There was a time when getting a "record deal" was the Holy Grail of music business success. Today, though, with independent artists having options that weren't available to them (or anybody else) before, getting a record deal isn't the same as it once was.

Things change. This is one of many good reasons to review your goals often. New opportunities and new circumstances come into your life constantly.

It's common for people to passively hold on to things from the past, even though circumstances in their lives (and their corresponding needs) have changed. Is this the case for you?

Don't shut things out. Adding "or something better" to the end of all your goals will keep options open.

The Ability to Start Now (Even if You're Afraid)

There is never a perfect time to do anything. Start now.

Don't let the fact that you don't know enough or that not everything is in order keep you from doing something. Real learning happens in the field—when you're out there making things happen. There is no "perfect time" or "better time" to get started. Also, so very often, things you think need to come together before you feel sure it's time to get started won't happen the way you had hoped it would.

Thinking about making an album doesn't touch people or change their lives. It doesn't make you money either.

So, start now, work out the kinks as you go, and make things happen!

For example, you can ...

- Put a video on YouTube right now.

- Book a show.

- Record something on your computer.

Time Management Skills

What kind of tasks should you focus on? The ones that will make you money (such as selling albums), get you in front of people (such as playing shows), or otherwise increase the value of your music and brand in a way that is both specific and measurable.

You can find these tasks by asking yourself three questions:

- Will I get money (in the form of cash, check or bank deposit) for doing this?

- Will I get more money (in the form of cash, check, or bank deposit) in the future for doing this?

- Will I get more fans (the kind who give me money) for doing this?

Note that the questions didn't ask whether you THINK you'll get more money or fans. You don't want opinions here; you want answers that are specific and measurable.

Business (and Personal) Support

The music business is much more fun, and things flow a lot more easily, when you have people to share the experience with!

You will benefit by having two distinct support groups:

- **Business Support** – This group is made up of people you can call on when you need business assistance, whether it's an answer to a business-related question, an introduction to somebody in the business, or assistance in accomplishing a business-related goal.

- **Personal Support** – This group is made up of people who know you outside the business and can give you perspective on non-business things. These are the people who "talk you off the ledge" when things get crazy, let you know when you're being an idiot, and will still talk to you, even if nobody in the music business will.

Your personal support group may be made up of family or friends who know you on a personal level. Or, it may be made up of people you are not closely attached to, as sometimes they are better able to see problems in your life to which you may be too close to see clearly.

For many people, the ultimate in business support comes from a group known as a "mastermind." You've done something similar, even without knowing it, if you've ever brainstormed promotion ideas with members of your band, chatted about good opportunities with other musicians after an open mic, or co-written a song.

Napoleon Hill first coined the term "mastermind group" in his seminal book, *Think and Grow Rich*. Hill described the group as: "… two or more minds working actively together in perfect harmony towards a common definite objective."

To put it in more simple terms: When you have multiple people, each with different experiences and specialized knowledge, coming together to solve a single problem, you are more likely to find a positive solution. Whether you need to find the best way to get 200 people to your next gig or get a demo of your new song to Barbra Streisand, a mastermind group will help.

A Supportive Infrastructure

What things do you need to have in place so that you'll be able to be successful in music?

At the core of this will be you. What do you have to do to make sure you're able to function properly? What do you need to eat? How much sleep do you need? What things should you stay away from?

Beyond this will be things like where you need to live, the type of transportation you need to conduct your business, and the skills you will need to have in place to be successful.

For example, if you find it's easier to write songs in a quiet space that is free from distractions like a television, radio, or family members, but you don't have a quiet room you can use, perhaps you should consider renting a small space away from home.

If you drink too much when you're at a bar and doing so keeps you from being in top form at rehearsals the next day, the best solution may be to, rather than attempt moderation, completely avoid bars.

It's your job to take care of yourself the best way you can so you're able to maintain the stamina it takes to have a thriving career in music.

The bottom line: If it will help you get where you want to go, do it.

Distraction Management

With all the talk about music piracy killing this industry, it's easy to overlook the far greater threat: distraction. Whether it's a job, a nagging spouse, or a bad habit, distraction has the potential to stop your career before it ever starts.

Distractions related to other people are usually the easiest to spot. Self-imposed or internal distractions can be more difficult to deal with.

You'll want take care of common interruptions by:

- turning off your phone
- turning off the television
- getting away from the computer
- getting away from other people

Doing these things will allow you to have greater focus on your music and get more (and better) work done.

What about activities that seem like a good idea?

For example, what about checking out other bands?

Seems like a perfectly reasonable thing to want to see what other acts are doing. Maybe you'll get some good ideas for new things to do on stage or how to keep the crowd engaged, right?

Or maybe checking out other bands is an activity that is limiting the time you have available for high-value activities, such as writing songs for your upcoming album, rehearsing, or playing a show of your own.

Look at how you're spending your time, energy, and resources.
Be honest about what's really keeping you from moving forward.

Remember what I wrote about managing your time: *when it comes to activities for your music business, everything you do should increase the value of your music and brand in a way that is both specific and measurable.*

If you want to go check out other bands, make the commitment to walk away from the evening with (at least) three new things to incorporate in your own show. Don't just passively watch and call what you're doing "work."

Again, focus on tasks that make money ... not those you think will make money and really don't get you any closer to what you want to do with your music or your music business goals.

IS THIS A DREAM?

Most people would rather participate in something than just watch it ... or so they'll tell you. But watching something is easier.

Television shows such as *American Idol, X Factor, The Voice,* etc. take a music career and strip it down to its most basic level, without showing anything beyond the facade being presented. There are no long rehearsals, creative (or other) disputes with band members, financial sacrifices, or any of the "non-fun" stuff. Because of this, it's not an accurate depiction of what people in the music business *really* experience.

A real career in the music business, or even simply learning to sing or play an instrument, takes work. You know that.

Many musicians have the fantasy that:

- You'll be "discovered" on YouTube.

- A record company executive will be driving his car through your small town, on a street in front of the club where you play, on the night of your bimonthly gig. Just before you're about to go on stage, he'll have a flat tire and be waiting for AAA outside. He'll hear you from the parking lot, come in, record contract in hand, and sign you on the spot.

- You'll sell the 1,000 CDs you just pressed ... without doing anything to make it happen.

- You'll get a random call asking you to join your favorite act.

- A popular artist will visit your website, hear your song, and record it.

Can these things happen?

Yes! From time to time, musicians get discovered or find success in the most unexpected, random ways. For example, these acts were all discovered on YouTube:

- Jessie J

- Justin Bieber

- Priscilla Renea

- Charice

- Arnel Pineda (current lead singer for the band Journey)

Other examples:

- Tim Owens fronted an Ohio-based, Judas Priest tribute band called British Steel. In 1996, after Rob Halford left Judas Priest, Owens stepped in as their lead singer.

- Tommy DeCarlo was working at The Home Depot. He had never been in a band. He was a fan of Boston and put recordings of himself singing over karaoke tracks of their songs on his Myspace page. Band leader Tom Schulz's wife heard DeCarlo's recordings and played them for her husband. In 2007, after the band's lead singer, Brad Delp, committed suicide, he approached DeCarlo to take over.

- Benoît David worked fixing damaged upholstery during the day and played in a Yes tribute band at night. While repairing seats on a boat, he got a call from Yes's bass guitarist, Chris Squire, who had researched him via online videos and Yes fan sites and wanted him to join the band.

The idea of instant stardom is alluring and adds an element to a musician's story that gets people's attention. Watching the newfound success of a Cinderella-esque musician plucked from obscurity is just as much a fascination for the general public as it is a deep-seated fantasy for many musicians.

The "dream" of being discovered, if it actually happens, can sell a lot of music. This is because most non-musicians have similar dreams, such as the dream of winning the lottery.

As a musician actually working in the music business, it's up to you to keep shiny objects in perspective. It's great to stay open to "instant fame" opportunities, such as an invitation to be on a reality television show, but don't neglect the "non-fantasy" investment of time, resources, and effort. While it's possible to get discovered like any of the acts mentioned above, your odds of successfully building and maintaining a long-lasting career are much better when you take a more pragmatic route.

While I would never deter you (or anyone) from aspiring to create success in whatever way you feel led to pursue, I encourage you to take control of your career and play a game you can most easily win. Come up with a plan that relies more on skill and dedication than luck.

Building a foundation for your career means that when the public moves on from the latest popular website or the latest YouTube viral music video is forgotten, you will still have a devoted fan base that will follow you no matter what is going on in the music industry.

WHAT WILL HAPPEN TO THE PHONE SEX GIRLS?
(HINT: The same thing that is happening to musicians!)

I once knew a woman who, during the day, worked as a teacher. She was extremely intelligent and great with her students. She was shy and quiet.

She also had a part-time job working as a phone sex operator.

By working a few evenings per week, she was able to make more money than she did at her full-time teaching job. It was an easy gig, and she could do it anonymously.

But things changed for phone sex operators when technology moved from a simple telephone to the use of webcams, where customers could actually see the women they were talking to. Phone calls started to decline and the demand for webcam performances increased. If a woman working in the phone sex business wanted to continue making a lot of money, she could no longer be just an anonymous voice.

This was an opportunity—for those who were willing to be seen.

The women who went with the trend, risking their anonymity by putting themselves on video, made a lot more money than they did by simply talking on the phone. Not only because that service commanded higher prices, but also because there were fewer people to compete for the same business.

Being a musician is the same way.

In today's music business, you can't get away with "half exposure" like you once could. Gone are the times of "exclusive" interviews, selling millions of records based on radio alone, and limited performances. Today, if you want to reach people, you have to do more work than in the past.

"Not playing it safe" doesn't mean you have to do everything that comes your way. But you need to be smart enough to know when you have a good opportunity ahead of you. Unfortunately, this isn't always as easy as it sounds, because the business is changing all the time.

Here is the litmus test:

Will the opportunity allow fans to connect with you in a new and more personable way?

If the answer is yes, do it.

MTV was a game changer. Lots of acts that were doing well in the late '70s but decided not to be "video friendly" died off quickly. Others, perhaps not as talented in terms of musical skill, because they were able to embrace the medium, with both interviews and music videos, quickly found themselves doing better than ever.

YouTube—because it allows for free (to you) and filterless distribution of MTV-style music videos and other video content—was a game changer. Those who got in early, before all the noise (free and filterless works for everybody), had a substantial advantage that no longer exists today.

Things like this are happening right now. Keep your eyes open and jump in when you see something will further the relationships and connection you have with your fans!

PARALYZED MUSICIANS

Releasing an album, making a video, or playing a gig can be scary. When you do, you open yourself up for criticism, which can especially sting when it's personal or about something you've put so much effort into creating.

This aspect of the business is so scary that it keeps most people paralyzed. These people call themselves musicians and always seem to be "in the studio" but never actually take the plunge by releasing anything in a big way, performing live, or promoting themselves.

You may be one of these people. If so, I hope the following story shows you that, while a facade can work for a little while, in the end, people would rather have something authentic and honest over something fabricated, even if it's not perfect.

An "Unmarketable" Talent

In 1990, C+C Music Factory released "Gonna Make You Sweat (Everybody Dance Now)," which soon hit number one on the Billboard Hot 100 in the United States and charted around the world in countries like Australia, Sweden, France, New Zealand, Norway, and Germany. The album of the same name has sold over 5,000,000 copies in the U.S. alone.

It was a massive hit. If you turned on MTV in 1991, you saw the video, which featured vocalists Freedom Williams and Zelma Davis, in heavy rotation.

But nowhere did you hear Zelma Davis, because she didn't actually sing on the record. The lead female vocal was actually recorded by Martha Wash.

Not only was Martha Wash absent from the video, she also didn't receive credit on the album. When the act went on tour, she wasn't invited to participate.

What happened? The producers, although they loved her voice, thought Wash was "unmarketable" due to her large size.

"Going to Make You Sweat (Everybody Dance Now)" was a huge hit that sold millions of copies when it was released, but that success was short-lived. Today, C+C Music Factory, more or less, exists in name only. It includes only one original member from the 1990s lineup that everybody knows, making it *very* close to a cover/tribute band of itself. "Everybody Dance Now" is a pop culture cliché.

"Facade" may look good, but it rarely has longevity.

IT DOESN'T HAVE TO BE PERFECT

Today, fans expect artists to be more accessible than ever. They want to connect with something they feel is "real," even if it's not perfect.

But beware of being too accessible and forgetting standard rules of etiquette.

John Mayer is a great example of both the pros and cons of "not perfect" social media. At one time, he was communicating via at least seven online outlets, including a Myspace page, a blog at his official site, another at Honeyee.com, one at Tumblr.com, and a photo blog at StunningNikon.com. He was one of the most-followed persons on Twitter, with 3,700,000 followers at one time.

Not only did John Mayer post about career-related matters; he also posted jokes, videos, photos, personal beliefs, and information about his everyday activities. He did almost everything himself, not through a publicist or other media professional.

This was engaging. Fans were interested. The media was interested.

Then John Mayer seemed to forget the basic rules of social etiquette. He told stories about ex-girlfriends, got into flame wars with other social media users, and used racial slurs.

And that's when social media backfired.

At that point he deleted everything, saying, "No artwork created by someone with a healthy grasp of social media thus far has proven to be anything other than disposable."

True, but note that, today, he's back on social media in moderation— perhaps the most healthy grasp of all.

In the end, even though John Mayer's use of social media (and media in general) hasn't been perfect, his career has greatly benefitted. His mistakes have both stimulated discussion and, perhaps surprisingly, allowed people to feel even more connected, as it's easier to see the humanity in somebody who isn't flawless.

This is what you're competing with.

THE MAGIC BULLET TO ENSURE SUCCESS IN MUSIC

If there is such a thing as a "magic bullet" in this business, this is it:

Build an audience.

Once you have an audience, you can do just about anything.

When you commit to having a career in the music business, what you're also committing to is building your audience. When you commit to that audience—by staying in touch with them and providing them value—they will be committed to you.

I believe that every musician who stays in this business for any length of time has the opportunity to cultivate a strong audience. You do this by applying three rules:

- Love them.

- Respect them.

- Provide them value.

That's it. Do these three things, and you're in.

But it gets even better …

At times, your audience will be bigger than others. People change, tastes change, and circumstances change, which can work for you or against you in terms of numbers. How many people in your audience do you really need to make a great living, though?

Not as many as you'd think.

You've probably heard the "1,000 True Fans" theory, which says you can make a pretty good living if you've got 1,000 people spending $100/year with you.

1,000 x $100/each = $100,000

But what would happen if you focused on developing 500 "superfans" who would spend

$300/year with you?

500 x $300/each = $150,000

You've just increased your income by 50 percent, even though you have only half as many fans.

What if you could do both, though? What if you could have "1,000 True Fans" and another 500 "superfans," who spend much more than average?

What if you could have these relationships for 10 or more years?

You can. The secret is creating a solid foundation of relationships on which you can build upon.

And that starts with winning people over, one individual at a time.

It's not sexy, I know. It is, however, doable.

CONCLUSION

The difference between those who do well in this music business and those who don't comes back to commitment. If you want success bad enough, you'll find a way to overcome your fears and make it happen.

Get clear on what you want and then go after it with everything you've got. You will not fail.

CHAPTER 2:

CHOOSE YOUR PATH

Which of the following would you rather have?

Impact

or ...

Ease

These are the two ways to approach your music career. Neither is better than the other, but they are different and will affect your business choices as well as what people think about your music, both during and after your career.

Regardless of whether you approach your music career wanting impact or ease, strive for a mixture of ambition and contentment. You want to have both—to be content with and have appreciation for where you are now—but, given that you want to reach as many people as possible with your art, be ambitious enough to see that through.

Whether you're going to change the world with your music or just make people feel good, you need a certain level of ambition in order to do it. However, you'll never be truly happy until you find contentment within yourself and begin forging out a career on your terms, based on your needs, wants, and goals.

IMPACT

In the music business, "impact" is a word often associated with music acts like Elvis Presley, The Beatles, Bruce Springsteen, Prince, Eminem, Aretha Franklin, Led Zeppelin, and Nirvana, who have seemingly affected millions of people at once. The impact most independent acts make, while just as powerful to the people affected, happens in a much different way—a single person at a time.

Impact is a Christian band leading somebody to follow Jesus. It's what happens when a girl with an eating disorder hears a song about loving yourself and finds the courage to get help. Also, impact is the change a kid undergoes when he becomes vegetarian after attending a "straightedge" show.

The ability to affect people in big ways is not always instant. It requires rapport, connection, and trust that, more often than not, are developed over a period of months or even years.

Impact requires both timing and tenacity, but you only have to worry about the latter. If you show up every day and do your work, the timing happens automatically.

While it's good to think about the impact you want to have, it should never be your primary focus. If you continue to write, record, and perform music that listeners connect with and that makes them feel good when they listen to it, the impact you're seeking to have will take care of itself.

Questions to ask yourself:

- How do you want to be remembered?

- What causes are you passionate about?

- Do you want to be known for more than just your music?

Dictionary.com defines "impact" as "the striking of one thing against another; forceful contact; collision."

If you're going to have impact, you're going to have to be bold. Anything less won't have the "forceful contact" against the status quo.

Wanting to make an impact is a defining choice you can make. However, it's the smaller choices that will follow that really determine whether you actually do make an impact.

As an example, if you're an artist who wants to make an impact by bringing attention to a local political or social issue, it's the smaller choices, such as whether to play a benefit show to bring attention to the issue, or not playing the show to keep from possibly alienating some of your fans, that will be meaningful.

Don't have the goal of making an impact for the sake of popularity. Your fans will sense whether you're being real or not. Look at acts that have had great impact and model them. Many of them didn't have the intention of making an impact; they simply were unafraid to be true to themselves and stayed true to a very specific musical vision while not giving in to ease.

To have greater impact in your music career:

- **Know Who You Are** – Acts that have impact embrace who they are and are comfortable with themselves. Then they make everything bigger, bolder, and louder.

- **Take Action First** – Don't wait to be recognized, don't ask for permission, and don't follow trends.

- **Take Risks** – Like gambling, the biggest payoffs in music are for those who take the biggest risks. If you play it too safe, you'll never win.

- **Set the Pace** – Most people are lazy and sluggish. If you wait for them to set the pace, you'll never get anywhere.

- **Keep People Guessing** – Giving your audience the same thing every time is comfortable, but it's not stimulating. Change up what you're doing to be more interesting and keep people's attention.

For maximum impact, you'll need to be original. This means you'll be creating something new. That can be a tough sell.

People aren't always open to "new." We want what we're used to, because it's comfortable. If you're doing something different, something that asks people to open to a new experience, or something that makes people uncomfortable, expect some resistance.

Do fans want something new and exciting?

They'll say they do. But this is another case of the difference between what people say and what people do.

The majority of times, people want something familiar.

Does McDonald's have the best hamburgers?

Does Starbucks have the best coffee?

Does Pizza Hut have the best pizza?

Most people would say no. Yet, respectively, these are the most popular hamburger, coffee, and pizza places.

Just like the majority of people who eat out, the majority of music fans have extreme inertia. It's easier for us to keep listening to the same thing we've always listened to than to try something new, because trying something new is risky.

It's usually tough to get momentum going in your favor when you're facing a mindset like this. You experience resistance almost every step of the way.

Should you choose to focus on making an impact, know that help, if you get any, will initially be minimal. This is because the comfort zone of the people you're trying to engage with will be working against you.

The people you're trying to win over aren't bad; they're simply working with old habits, limited time, and limited energy. They have more to lose by taking a risk on you than not doing anything.

So that's what most will do: nothing. It doesn't matter that your music is better, you're more engaging, and you have something more entertaining.

When your goal is to make an impact, you're not just battling the usual career obstacles that you'd have in any worthy goal; you're also battling the habits and preferences of potential fans, who usually aren't so quick to see the greatness of what you're doing.

The good news is that enthusiasm is contagious and the "risk" of trying something new is lessened with each person you win over. As you keep going on this route and prove to others that you have something worthwhile, more and more people will join the cause and come along to help you. Things will get easier with each step, because the workload will be shared by more and more people.

Things won't get really easy until you're at the top of the mountain. At that point, you've proved to everything working against you that you have something of value. It's not just subjective anymore. Not everybody will like the music, but they won't be able to argue that you haven't made an impact.

The music you release is now the "safe" choice to listen to, and your career, even though it might not stay at its peak for long, will be long and easy.

Going for "impact" in the music business isn't for the faint of heart. It will require you to be extremely clear on the vision for your act. You'll need to keep focused on what you want, as many of the people you come in contact with will want to change it in order to shortcut the process it takes to sell a lot of music.

While you may never change the business, like Elvis Presley, The Beatles, or Nirvana, your music can have just as much impact on the individuals who hear it. Focus on affecting one person at a time for maximum results.

EASE

Every band knows the best way to get a quick audience is to play cover songs. This is the ultimate example of choosing "ease" as a career approach.

Covers let you take advantage of the people who've come before you. Doing this will allow you to start way ahead of bands who are trying for impact. Rather than working against the system to turn people onto a new style of music, you're working with it, giving an audience that already exists music that they already enjoy.

With this route, there is no boulder being pushed up the mountain. That work has already been done by acts that have made an impact: the bands you are covering. In fact, not only is there no boulder to push, the trail is a lot smoother, since it has already been blazed.

But where does the path take you?

You'll make money fast. Nothing wrong with that.

You may get on the radio. Nothing wrong with that.

You'll probably sell records, get people to your shows, and do pretty well. Nothing wrong with that.

So what's the problem?

The path to the top may be quick, but it drops off suddenly. It's what I call a "heart attack curve." Everything peaks out at some point … then you're dead.

Why? You're a commodity with little or nothing to differentiate you from other acts following the same path.

Harry Connick Jr. sounds like Frank Sinatra, not the other way around.

And ask yourself ...

Is the average guy on the street more likely to be aware of AC/DC or Jackyl?

This isn't to say that "ease" doesn't work well or pay big. Michael Bublé has played it safe, and there are plenty of middle-aged women who love him for just that reason.

You always know what you'll get when you buy a Michael Bublé album, because he doesn't deviate from a very specific formula. Assuming you like formula, you'll never be disappointed.

Michael Bublé is the McDonald's of the music business:

- Songs (and arrangements) that have already been hits

- Frank Sinatra's image

- A consistent formula that works—fans know what they're getting every time

Michael Bublé found a great niche, and he's made a ton of money.

But answer this question: When all you do are "safe" cover songs, what's keeping somebody else from knocking you off?

Nothing.

Don't worry about this. You can (and should) expect others to do just what you did.

When you choose this path, your job isn't to innovate; your job is it to copy.

Speed is your biggest asset. You want to take a "low-hanging fruit" and build something as quickly as possible.

If you're trying to jump on a current trend, you will need to be flexible and willing to change. You're not blazing your own trail; you're following somebody else's. So when something changes, go with it.

Just because you're currently playing a certain style of music doesn't mean you can't switch to something else. Many successful acts have switched genres in the middle of their careers and gone on to greater success than before.

Michael Bolton started out as a hard rock singer, but is best known for the soft rock ballads he recorded years later. Sugar Ray, once a metal band, really hit after switching to pop. Katy Perry, known as Katy Hudson, was a Christian singer.

In some cases, switching genres has actually led acts to not only success, but also impact. For example, Ministry started as a new-wave, synth-pop act, changing a few years later to industrial metal, a much harsher and more aggressive genre in which they're considered innovators.

While going for "ease" is great in theory and works for many, you may find it actually easier to forget the low-hanging fruit, create the music that you want, and win people over with the sheer force of your enthusiasm. Being engaged in your work, even if the job is technically a harder one, goes a long way toward happiness.

HOW TO CHOOSE YOUR PATH

You probably already know which path is for you, but if not, here's how to decide:

If you want to make money fast, go with the "ease" route. If you want career longevity and more money in the long run, you're much better off blazing your own trail and letting people come behind you.

Is there a middle ground? Sure. For example, you could be like Pat Boone and do covers of great songs in a totally different style.

But the more you go for ease, the less impact you'll have. Pat Boone, with his clean-cut image, initially sold more copies of "Tutti Frutti" than Little Richard did. According to Billboard, he was the second biggest charting artist of the late 1950s, coming in behind Elvis Presley.

But who has had the most impact?

In the end, the choice of impact vs. ease is a spectrum more than an "all or nothing" decision. The more you have of one, the less you'll have of the other.

What you choose is personal. There is no "bad" decision, but I encourage you to stay away from a 50/50 mix. This is the ultimate in playing it safe, and, when that happens, nobody will be happy: you'll be too edgy for some and too safe for others. No one will get exactly what they want.

DON'T GET TOO COMFORTABLE

Regardless of whether you prefer impact to ease or vice versa, you'll want to be aware of (and keep a close eye on) perhaps the biggest enemy to your music business career: comfort. Comfort is so powerful that it can derail a career before it gets started.

Many talented people have given up their music business dreams to:

- please a significant other
- take a job with more "benefits"
- get off the road
- earn a "steady paycheck"
- have a normal life

All of these things are great. The problem is that they're not always compatible with a music career.

Even established musicians can fall prey to comfort. We've all seen artists who get "too comfortable" and take a nosedive when it comes to their art and business. This isn't because they've lost their talent; it's because they're following a creative formula that did work but no longer does.

This is easy to do, and it happens on both the music and business side of this industry. Perhaps the best industry-wide example is the transition from the "old-school" music business to where we are now. We saw it coming, little by little, but instead of working with that momentum of change, we went into denial about it. And when that didn't work, we fought the losing battle against it.

Why wouldn't we? The old-school music business had been around for 100+ years, and, for most of the people in the industry, it was all they knew.

In the old-school music business, we controlled the manufacture and distribution of the product. We controlled the media around the promotion of it. When the product broke (or we released it in a new format), people had to buy another one.

It was perfect. And it worked … until it didn't. At that point, it couldn't be fixed, because it had already been changed significantly.

While it may not be as drastic as the changes the music business has seen in the last couple of decades, the changes that are happening within your business can be just as disruptive.

GETTING USED TO CHANGE

A skill that will help you to be more comfortable with the changing aspects of both art and business is to become more comfortable with change in your daily life.

How do you do this? Force change just enough so you get outside your comfort zone, but not so much that you get into "panic mode" and start making irrational decisions.

"Panic mode" is what happened when the old-school music business changed. People in the industry weren't paying attention, so when the new model of digital distribution (and everything else that came with it) took hold, they started doing irrational things, like suing their best customers or, at the very least, trying to scare them.

Not good.

When change happens in life, you're much better off staying cool and being rational. Your capacity to do this happens as you increase your capacity to handle change.

How do you do this?

Start simple. As they say, "Little hinges swing big doors."

If you like your coffee with cream, take it black. Order onion rings instead of French fries. Take the stairs instead of an elevator.

If you play in a rock band, take an acoustic gig. If you perform solo, play with a full band. If you never perform live, take any gig!

If you're a songwriter who normally writes on piano, write on guitar. Or write over an existing track. If you're used to writing solo, do a co-write.

Does this sound simple? If so, take things up a notch. And do it again, and again, and again. Every day, making the decision that, "I will do something today that expands my comfort zone."

Why?

The reason we develop habits is that we've had success with something.

There's nothing wrong with that, but having a habit for too long, to the point where it becomes unconscious, can be detrimental to your health, well-being, and music business success.

"If you want to keep getting what you're getting, keep doing what you're doing."

There is some truth to this, and it applies in some situations, but very rarely does it apply to the music business. This is because the music business is constantly changing.

And this is why you want to be comfortable with change.

7 WAYS TO GET OUT OF YOUR COMFORT ZONE AND START TAKING RISKS

1. **Work Yourself Up** – Start where you are and work yourself up to bigger things. "Success" means forming the habit of taking risks and totally embracing "growth over comfort."

   A baby learns to crawl, and then stand, before he learns how to walk. The first steps are shaky but get smoother and steadier with time.

   A guitar player learns in a similar fashion. At first the playing is clunky, but with practice, it eventually smooths out.

   Are you approaching things in a way that is keeping you "crawling" instead of something more? If so, work to embrace more risks, even if they're small, to expand your comfort zone.

2. **Do It Daily** – When you do something daily, it keeps you from putting something off until tomorrow, because you'll also be doing it tomorrow.

   Will you be a better musician if you practice one hour daily or seven hours one day per week? If you know the answer to this, you know the power of daily practice.

3. **Start Something** – You need to go first. Don't wait for other people to join you, even if it's just the people in your band.

   Grunge music was popular in 1991. Nobody cared about the grunge bands who came along in 1996.

   When you go first, you set the pace.

4. **Be Willing to Fail** – Your biggest lessons will be from failure. Remember, if you don't "crash the car," you'll never know how fast it can go.

   The best way to learn a new language is to speak it. You'll never do that if you're worried about making mistakes.

   Similarly, the best musicians are the ones who aren't afraid to take risks when they're playing. Do you want to be good? If so, you have to play, and playing means you risk making mistakes.

5. **Be an Observer** – This habit isn't so you can judge yourself; it's so you can push yourself out of your comfort zone and grow. Be an observer: notice what works (and what doesn't), and keep tweaking what you do so it gets better.

   When you're on stage, you have a different perspective of the performance than people in the audience do. Think of things from their perspective. Better yet, record yourself and watch and listen like they do.

6. **Own It** – If you're going to do something, you'd might as well go big. If you take a risk that doesn't work out, own it. It's not a risk if you don't take ownership.

   Ever seen a musician fall off stage? You can't act like it didn't just happen, so you'd might as well own it and have fun with it.

7. **Be Committed to the Process** – If you're constantly getting out of your comfort zone, by definition, it will never get easier.

   We are always changing. Nothing is static. As a musician, you know that when you perform, as no two performances are exactly the same, even if you perform the same material.

You're either getting better at what you do or getting worse. It might not be obvious, because the changes happen slowly and over a period of time, but when it comes to the anchors in your career (writing and recording a new album, going on tour), you'll notice.

Commit to the process, and you'll always be moving in the right direction.

THE MYTH OF THE OVERNIGHT SUCCESS

People who have won a big lottery prize (between $50,000 and $150,000) are twice as likely to file bankruptcy than the general population. That's what a 2010 paper published by researchers at Vanderbilt University, the University of Kentucky, and the University of Pittsburgh says.

The researchers in this study looked at two groups of lottery winners: those who won between $50,000 and $150,000 and those who won more modest prizes of $10,000 or less. Five years afterward, the big winners were the ones more likely to have filed for bankruptcy.

How is that possible?

Lack of financial literacy. In other words, these people simply lacked the skills to effectively handle money.

If you're looking to be wealthy, odds are that you'll be much more successful with a "get rich slow" method, such as consistent saving or investment, since doing things this way will allow you to develop the skills needed to keep that money.

The same concept applies to your music business.

We've all seen the "YouTube sensations," the reality show winners, and the one-hit wonders who seemingly come out of nowhere. They're everywhere. Then they vanish.

Why?

Like most lottery winners, very few of the musicians who come out of nowhere with viral videos or promotion thanks to mass media have the things needed to keep that momentum going.

Things like:

- more than one good song or funny video

- knowledge of who their fans are or what motivates them to take action

- the experience to know what works (and what doesn't) when it comes to marketing music

These are the things that automatically come with time while you're working on getting noticed. So while it might seem like there are periods in your career where absolutely nothing is happening, the skills you're learning during these times are actually some of the most important ones you'll need to help you forge a long-lasting career.

For example, experience dealing with the media, building long-lasting fan relationships, and doing business tasks are all skills you will need for a sustainable music career. You don't automatically get these when you have success straight out of the gate. The majority of the time, they are earned through hard work—usually during the early stage of a career.

For an up-and-coming artist, every media opportunity is important. Even the small, seemingly insignificant interviews are what will prepare you to handle the future interviews that will be seen or heard by a large audience. Like what an open mic night or talent show is to performing on stage, an interview on a small podcast or radio or television station is a great place to learn what works and what doesn't when it comes to working with media.

Want to see something painful? Some of the best examples of interviews gone wrong are YouTube sensations and reality show contestants who, without any training or experience, suddenly find themselves on major talk shows like *Ellen*, whatever Anderson Cooper is doing, or *Live! with Kelly and Michael.*

Be thankful you have the opportunity to get your media skills together before the whole world is watching.

Beyond developing the skills to work with media, as a "get rich slow" artist working your way up, you learn how to work with and develop relationships with fans. Fans are the foundation for a solid career, and your relationships with them are paramount for a long-lasting career.

Like any relationship, the best relationships with fans are those built over time. While a big radio hit can bring a lot of people to your shows or sell a lot of albums in a short amount of time, long music careers happen when fans have an opportunity to experience your music in several different ways, over a long period of time.

For example, if a fan hears your music at a high school dance, sees you play live while in college, then hears you again a few years later at a wedding, your music is being attached to several memories this person has. That is much more powerful than hitting big via a television show or short-lived radio hit, where you and your music connect in a very limited way.

Going about your career in a slow and steady way also lets you learn various business skills you might not have the opportunity to learn if, at the very beginning of your career, everything suddenly takes off. This will help you to hire quality people for these jobs when you eventually start to outsource them, because, having done the jobs yourself, you'll be able to assess who is capable of doing them.

There are exceptions to every rule. While there have been some very successful artists born from reality television shows and contests like *American Idol* who have gone on to build strong music careers, this is not the norm. If a long-term music career is your goal, you'll have a better chance of achieving it through slow and consistent improvement over time than through anything else.

RESILIENCE

*"My overnight success was really 15 years in the making.
I'd been writing songs since I was six and playing in bands
and performing since I was 14."*

– Lisa Loeb

We live in an age of what seems to be instant celebrities. But just because we have fast-track promotion options like reality television shows, viral videos, and sex tapes doesn't mean it's a good idea to take advantage of them.

While these opportunities do work for some, you'll have much better odds of success by possessing these three things:

- **Quality Songs** – The National Songwriters Association has a saying: "It all begins with a song." A song is your foundation to build upon. A great one will allow you to create a career that lasts a lifetime. Average songs get lost ... quickly.

  Don't have quality songs? If you can't figure out how to write some, find somebody who can.

- **Quality Performance** – On any given night, there are tens of thousands of acts playing in bars, clubs, and other venues across the world. Most are forgettable. Those who aren't stick with you. Remember what they did? Do that.

- **Quality Connection** – In the end, whether you're a pop singer, a church musician, or a dance club DJ, your success depends entirely on how well you connect with your audience.

Legendary sales copywriter Robert Collier once said that the secret of successful advertising copy is "entering the conversation already taking place in the customer's mind."

Connection via music is similar.

Connection with an audience happens when people feel you "get" them. They have problems, dilemmas, and dreams that you understand, and that understanding comes through in every note of the songs you play and every movement you make on stage.

None of these things happen instantly. They are skills acquired over years of trial and error. Master them, though, and you'll have years of return.

The companies and products we consider "household names" didn't happen because of luck; they happened because of resilience.

Amazon.com launched in 1994 but didn't post a profit until 2001.

Angry Birds was Rovio's 52nd game.

WD-40 stands for "Water Displacement—40th Attempt."

Soichiro Honda, founder of Honda Motor Company, was turned down for an engineering job at Toyota and, after starting his own company, lost a contract to supply Toyota with piston rings due to poor quality.

Akio Morita, founder of Sony Corporation, sold fewer than 100 units of Sony's first product, a rice cooker.

And the same can be said for many successful people in the entertainment industry ...

In Fred Astaire's first screen test, the testing director of MGM noted: "Can't act. Can't sing. Slightly bald. Can dance a little."

Legendary Los Angeles club owner Bill Gazzarri turned down Van Halen for being "too loud."

In 1954, Elvis Presley was fired from the Grand Ole Opry after just one appearance, with the recommendation that he resume his truck driving career.

Decca Records rejected The Beatles, saying that "guitar groups are on the way out" and "the Beatles have no future in show business."

Igor Stravinsky's *The Rite of Spring* provoked a riot during its premiere.

There is no success without failure, and the only way to move beyond failure is resilience.

5 Traits That Help Build Resilience

1. **A Solid Support Network** – If you're in the music business long enough and taking the risks you should be taking, you're going to take a few punches and have to deal with criticism from others, such as when you release new music.

   Perhaps the most negative thing of all is what you'll have to deal with in terms of your own internal criticism, which often keeps music from ever being released.

   The solution? A solid support network of friends, family, and business associates can help you to create the foundation needed to deal with these and other similar issues.

2. **Finding Positive Meaning in "Failure"** – Not everything you try will work. If you release enough music, not all of it will go over well. If you play enough shows, not all of them will have lots of people in the audience.

   The more quickly you find out what doesn't work, the more quickly you can do something that does.

3. **The Ability to Make a Good Decision (and Stick With It)** – The quicker you're able to make a good decision and the better your ability to stick with that decision, the more in control of your situation you'll be. Ignore something and a decision will be made for you.

   Situation: You're in a band with people you can't get along with.

Good Decision: Leaving on your terms, while you still have a choice.

4. **Taking Responsibility for Everything** – If your guitar gets stolen before your gig, is it your fault? Don't spend time worrying about that. It's your responsibility to get another one before the show.

5. **A Higher Purpose** – Whether you're using music to bring people to Jesus, be a good example for your kids, or raise money so you can help starving kids, having a reason you do things will help you to get through the frustrating parts of your music business journey.

Every successful person has had more failures than successes. If you want success, fail fast and fail often. Choose your path, create a solid foundation on which to build your success, and get going. As long as you stay the course, everything else will work itself out.

Success in the music business is, for the most part, a slow and gradual process. Still, for those who wish to speed things up, there are ways to do so. You won't get quick results without pushing yourself in a big way though.

The only way to get really good at anything quickly is to completely immerse yourself in it. The music business is no exception.

The best way to completely jump in is to "clear the decks" and go for it. That means quitting other obligations, such as a day job, and going full time with music. Without a backup plan to bring in money, you'll get good at finding ways to earn money through your music, because if you don't, you won't be eating.

If you need motivation to hit the road, book a show in New York City and another, 30 days later, in Los Angeles. Book gigs along the way to fill the space between.

Tied down because of home ownership or a rental agreement? Finding somebody to stay in your place will force you to stay on the road.

Looking for something not as drastic? Say "yes" to a gig opportunity this weekend, even if you're not 100 percent ready.

If you're in the process of putting together a band to play with, rather than waiting to get the lineup together, perform solo.

CONCLUSION

Time is going to pass regardless, so you might as well make the most of it. Get clear on where you want to go, then make it happen.

You will fail along the way. If you're not failing, you're not working hard enough. If you look for positive meaning in failure and know why you're doing what you're doing, these "mistakes" won't be problems. They'll be lessons that will help you arrive at your destination that much faster.

CHAPTER 3:

PLAY YOUR GAME

Your music career doesn't just happen. Where you are now is the direct result of decisions you have made.

Want to be in a better place a year from now? Start making better decisions.

You are in control.

You set the pace. You take the risks. You get the rewards.

THE RECORD LABEL FANTASY

Nobody is going to care about your music career as much as you do. Because of this, turning everything over to a record label, management company, or anybody else is, at best, a way to end up going in a direction you're unhappy with or, at worst, a way to be completely derailed.

So why do so many musicians do this?

Perhaps the biggest reason is that the average musician has heard dozens of music business "success stories" that sound pretty good from the outside. This music business folklore, passed around for years from musician to musician, because it is so ubiquitous and because it takes advantage of our emotion surrounding this industry, is rarely questioned. Plus, to add to the confusion, some of it *is* true!

The old school music business has been around for decades. It's still something that a large number of musicians want to be part of.

Why? In many cases, it's the fantasy people have about record labels and what it means to be signed to one.

Many musicians believe that once they sign to a big record label, their work is over. In the record label fantasy, the only thing the musician does is record a good song. After that, everything is handled.

This means that the manager makes good management decisions, the agent gets the act good gigs, the label handles everything involved with selling lots of records, radio stations all agree how brilliant the single is and play the hell out of it, the press only writes great reviews, and the fans recognize the act's greatness and swear total allegiance.

In a record label fantasy, as long as a good song has been recorded, the musician will be successful. Nothing he does is wrong—*ever*. If the album tanks, it's somebody else's fault.

How did so many musicians come to have the same fantasy about how record labels operate? Because, as with many stereotypes and fantasies, the record label fantasy has elements of truth.

In the mid-twentieth century, when the modern music industry was really starting to take hold, options for promoting music were extremely limited. The big three were live performance, broadcast radio, and broadcast television.

Live performance was limited in its reach, due to the small size of most venues and technology limits on sound reinforcement at the time. Appearances by music acts on television were limited and often on variety shows that catered to the general public. The primary way for music to be heard by large numbers of people from a specific demographic was via radio.

And here is how it happened …

PAYOLA

In the 1950s, it was common to assign copyright from songs to
influential disc jockeys and others who helped to make those songs
popular. An example of this happened in 1955, when Chess Records
released "Maybellene" by Chuck Berry and assigned 1/3 of the writing
credit to disc jockey Alan Freed.

Not only was this common, it was also *legal* at the time. Freed also was
given cash by the label.

The song went on to sell over 1,000,000 copies, reaching number one
on Billboard's R&B chart and number five on the Pop chart.

Marshall Chess, the son of Chess founder Leonard Chess, later said
of the deal, "He [Freed] played the hell out of Chuck's first record,
'Maybellene,' because of that. My father says he made the deal, and by
the time he got to Pittsburgh, which was half a day's drive away, my
uncle back at home was screaming, 'What's happening? We're getting
all these calls for thousands of records!'"

That *was* the power of radio. If you played a song enough times, you'd
sell records.

And with money on the line, disc jockeys made sure a song received
enough airplay to get sales and chart. As an example, because of this
deal, one night, Freed played "Maybellene" for two hours straight
during his show on WINS in New York.

Who could afford this kind of promotion? Record labels.

By 1960, this practice, known as "payola," was all but gone—at least in
the open. It continued to exist via third-party, independent promoters
who sidestepped FCC regulations for almost 50 more years.

And the power of this type of activity continued to fuel the record label
fantasies of musicians who dreamed of being on the receiving end of
such massive promotion.

SPRAY AND PRAY

By the 1960s, with the recorded music industry bigger than ever, labels started signing more and more acts. Many used a method of promotion known as "spray and pray."

Just as a shotgun shoots several pellets at once, with only some of the pellets actually hitting the target, a "spray and pray" promotion model is based on releasing several artists during the same time. The more artists that are released, the greater the odds that *something* will hit.

This old-school record label business model, in many ways, is an all-or-nothing gamble for artists. You either hit it big, or, in most cases, you don't hit at all.

This business model still exists today, although it isn't nearly as common as it once was.

You've probably read interviews with artists who've said things like, "Well, I was on the same label as *(INSERT POPULAR ARTIST NAME HERE)*, and, because of this, my record never got the attention it deserved and it tanked."

That sort of sentiment reflects the "spray and pray" model at work.

Typically, a major label releases several albums in a limited way, watches for those that seem to take hold quickly, and only then does the needed work to make them successful.

With this strategy, albums have a very limited time to show potential, and if something doesn't hit almost instantly, it's common for labels to cut their losses, either letting the album tank or dropping the act from the label entirely. This allows them to focus on putting their resources into acts and albums they feel have better chances of making money.

While there are a lot of disappointed artists, in the end, the strategy works OK for labels. About 12 percent of albums make enough money so the 88 percent of albums that don't make money are covered.

Why would any musician take those odds?

For one, every musician, assuming he knows the odds, thinks he's an exception to the rule. For another, because it's the label that decides when to cut the cord, there is psychological security for musicians who want to blame something other than themselves when their projects fail.

MUSICIAN WINS LOTTO

I know a musician who went to New York to shop for a record deal. He was a great talent who had played everything on his demo.

As he made his rounds, he got very little interest. He was young, good looking, and very talented, but guys like that are a dime a dozen.

After he left one label, the A&R guy he had talked with took his press kit and threw it in the trash.

A secretary happened to see his photo in the wastebasket and thought, "This guy looks interesting." She grabbed his press kit and put it on her desk.

Another A&R guy walked by her desk and made a comment about it. "This guy was just in here," she told him. "He's looking for a deal."

That was all it took for him to get a second look—and a record deal.

The result was two Top 20 singles off his debut album, videos on MTV, a national tour, and a career that is still going strong. It was also the fulfillment of perhaps the biggest record label fantasy of all—a record deal, stardom, and a career from simply walking into a record label office and submitting a press kit.

Was it a fluke?

Yes, it was a fluke. Half the success stories in music are flukes. I know a songwriter who got his song heard (and eventually cut) by going through a tour bus driver. I know another who did the same thing via an artist's hairdresser.

Fiona Apple got her record deal by giving a demo tape to a friend, who happened to be the babysitter of music publicist Kathryn Schenker. Schenker heard it being played, asked about it, kept the tape, and then passed it to Sony Music executive Andy Slater.

These synchronicities happen. But will they happen to you?

Since the modern music business was born, there have been artists who have "made it big" without doing the work you're probably already doing. As mentioned earlier, Tommy DeCarlo had never been in a band before joining Boston, and there are numerous stories of acts being signed without ever having played a live show.

William Hung signed a three-album deal after a failed American Idol audition. He sold over 200,000 albums.

Thanks to reality television and other similar opportunities, more and more artists are shortcutting the standard time and effort it takes for most acts to get record label and other entertainment company deals. As long as these shows exist and there is an audience interested in the people who appear on them, this will continue to happen.

Opportunities like this are fun to think about, but are they the kind of opportunities that you want?

In truth, you never know. You could end up in one of the greatest rock bands ever, or you could end up, like the majority of viral video and reality television musicians, on the same shelf as media train wrecks like "Balloon Boy" and "Octomom."

Like a lottery, it's possible to win the record label fantasy. But like a lottery, it's not likely.

Just as money put into lottery tickets is usually better invested in something else, the time you spend chasing the record label fantasy will likely be better invested elsewhere.

Here is the bottom line …

There is nothing wrong with signing a record deal and having dreams, but keep shiny objects and fantasy in perspective. The more work you're willing do early in your career, before you're ready for a record deal, the better record deal you'll be able to get when you are ready. And the more work you're willing to do after signing a deal, the better your odds of being successful.

HOW TO GET A RECORD DEAL

As much as it may seem like getting a record deal comes down to luck, fate, or something beyond your control, those on the inside know it has little to do with it.

Anybody can get a record deal. If this is something that's important to you, don't doubt that it's possible.

What's the secret? You need to know how to make the pitch and then be able to back it up with more than just promises.

The music business is changing. Broadcast radio is losing listeners to online services like Spotify, satellite radio like XM/Sirius, and mobile, iPod-type devices that can hold 20,000 or more songs (the average music library has 7,160 songs) with ease. There is increased competition from non-music entertainment and piracy.

These changes have led to a generally smarter industry. The old-school record company guys, although they still exist, are being forced out by a newer breed of music executive who isn't intimidated by new technology, has promotion skills that go beyond just radio, and understands what gets people to buy music, now that a traditional album purchase is optional for access.

The majority of record labels today aren't looking to sign artists they can control, but artists who will work alongside them to meet their goals. With competition from other labels, so many do-it-yourself business models as options, and artists doing so well on their own that they don't really need record deals, this is the only way labels can get quality acts.

Major labels are looking for two types of artists to sign:

1. Artists they can make money with.

2. Artists who satisfy emotional needs in ways money can't.

You want to be an artist who is both.

A label must make money to keep its doors open, so the ability to make money with your music is important. If you're looking for a record deal, though, make sure you keep focused on the emotional payment the label's workers receive, as this may be an even more important factor to you getting the support you need to both get the deal and make sure it's successful.

Emotional payment for somebody at a record label is the sense of pride when discovering and working with a great act, the attention received from being a tastemaker, and the feeling that comes from a job well done.

And that "emotional payment" brings everything back to music.

Music, for a true artist, is something that comes out of every pore of his body. This is what will not only make a record label money, but also give the people working there the satisfaction of working on "art" they can be proud of.

There is no denying a true artist when you see one. A true artist can bring a hush over a crowded and noisy bar. A true artist doesn't need fancy lights, smoke machines or other gimmicks. A true artist's work stands on its own, and it's powerful.

Beyond that, a true artist keeps going. He plays until the timer hits zero. He's "in the game" whether the game is going well or not.

This is the type of act record labels are looking for. They are the ones with which the people at the label get paid twice—money *and* emotional payoff.

There is nothing wrong with the "easy money" acts that labels sign, but if they have success, it's short lived and labels know this. Those with impact can earn a steady income for years, long after they peak.

TWO DIFFERENT ACTS WITH A SINGLE THING IN COMMON

Paris Hilton is famous for her inherited wealth and controversial lifestyle. In years past, she was thought to be one of the most provocative people in the world. Yet at the same time, thought to be one of the most boring.

Paris Hilton is a great example of "easy money" for a label. Because of who she is, getting the word out about any music she releases will be pretty easy, and she'll likely sell *some* records, but because she's not a musician or a singer, sales will drop off rather quickly.

Which is why Paris Hilton was dropped from her label shortly after her debut album was released.

Still, the album has sold 200,000 copies and reached 18 on the Billboard Hot 100. Not bad for a non-musician.

On the other hand, there is Meat Loaf.

Meat Loaf once compared his relationship to the music industry to that of a "circus clown." Although he'd had success with musicals, including *Rocky Horror Picture Show* and *Hair*, his traditional music career was slow to take off.

In 1971, Meat Loaf was signed to Motown but left the label when vocals from his favorite song recorded during his sessions there were replaced with new vocals by Edwin Starr. In 1976, he recorded lead vocals on Ted Nugent's *Free-for-All* album but only on five of nine tracks and only after original vocalist Derek St. Holmes quit the band.

During this time, Meat Loaf was with composer John Steinman, writing and recording something a bit closer to what he had previously excelled with: material based around a musical sci-fi update of *Peter Pan*. When it was done, the duo spent two and a half years auditioning for record labels.

Not everybody got it. Clive Davis rejected the project, saying, "Actors don't make records."

Todd Rundgren, upon hearing the material, claims he rolled on the floor laughing.

Then he said, "I've got to do this album. It's just so out there!"

Not only did he produce it, he also played lead guitar on it. Members of his band, Utopia, contributed their talents as well.

The result was *Bat Out of Hell*, one of the most popular albums in the history of recorded music.

- 43,000,000 units sold.

- On the Billboard charts for nine years.

- After 30+ years, it still sells 200,000 units annually.

The moral? Play your game.

PLAY YOUR GAME

Play your game. What does that mean?

It means you're in charge and you do music your way. That's the only music that has any kind of credibility and substance.

It means your music doesn't sound like what's being played on the radio because it isn't meant to sound like what's being played on the radio. Unless it *is* meant to sound like what's being played on radio, in which case you play the hell out of that type of music and don't apologize.

Either way, you set your own rules and let other people come to *your* table.

Here are examples of artists being true to form when it came to the decisions they made involving licensing their music:

Justin Timberlake is a pop musician. He follows trends and he's not so attached to his music that he's beyond licensing it. When McDonald's uses his song in commercials, nobody calls him a "sell-out," because for him, that isn't selling out.

When Gene Simmons shills the "KISS Kasket" (casket and beer cooler), nobody thinks anything of it, because that's what Gene Simmons does. The KISS name and logo have been licensed to over 3,000 products.

Would you turn down $50,000 to put your song in a commercial?

Sub Pop Records' The Thermals turned down $50,000 to allow its song "It's Trivia" to be used in a commercial.

DC-based band Trans Am turned down $180,000 for rights to the song "Total Information Awareness."

Why would bands turn down that much money? Because the company that wanted to use the songs was Hummer.

"We figured it was almost like giving music to the Army or Exxon," Philip Manley of Trans-Am told the Associated Press.

You can "play your game" any way you like, but you won't be successful or have any credibility if you constantly say one thing and do another. That only makes you look like a hypocrite.

Every successful entertainer knows this.

This simply means you can't please everybody. As the saying goes, "When you try to please everybody, you'll please nobody."

So please yourself, do what you do, and don't apologize.

Paris Hilton is not a serious musician. She released a fun album with catchy songs that had little to no depth, because that's in alignment with who she is.

The result? All things considered, she got pretty good reviews. Allmusic commented that her album was "more fun than anything released by Britney Spears or Jessica Simpson, and a lot fresher, too."

Meat Loaf is intense. He's the kind of guy who cries when he sees a greeting card commercial and throws tantrums when he doesn't get his way. He's not a soul musician that belongs on Motown; he's a "rock opera" singer who will jump into the audience and kick your ass if you taunt him.

Bat Out of Hell is an intense album. It's Meat Loaf in audio form.

In 1993, while looking back on the album, John Steinman said it was "timeless in that it didn't fit into any trend."

And it still hasn't been part of any trend.

"It's never been a part of what's going on," Steinman said. "You could release that record at any time and it would be out of place."

Like Meat Loaf, you may never be part of what's going on. Don't let that stop you from taking action.

Play *your* game.

THE DO-IT-YOURSELF RECORD COMPANY MODEL

All too often, independent acts are led down a path based on what they think everybody else is doing. They think that's the way the game is played, whether they like it or not.

Just because somebody else is getting their music out there in the seemingly "tried and true" way doesn't mean you have to follow. You are in control of how you run your business and live your life. If you don't like any aspect of the music business, simply change the environment to one where you call the shots. Or, as a poker player once told me, "If you don't like the game being played, change tables."

While there is value to the "standard practices" of the music industry that are based on years and years of trial and error, the industry is changing quickly. Just because something used to work doesn't mean it works now.

And just because something works for one person doesn't mean it will work for you. If you're doing things on your own, without the help of a major label, you'll need to modify what you've learned from the traditional business to create your own plan that works best for you.

If you choose the do-it-yourself route, getting your music to your fans is a three-step process:

1. Make the product.

2. Distribute the product.

3. Market the product.

How do you get all of this done? When you go indie, the short answer is, "Any way you can."

When you're in charge of your business, life is much simpler. You can do what you want, when you want.

For example, when you're the boss, there is no need to get the budget for your next record approved, because you're the one who makes the decisions on things like that. And who needs a budget when you've got all the needed equipment to put an album together via your computer?

Obviously, the things you can accomplish on your own compared to what you can accomplish with a major label behind you will differ, as you're likely dealing with different budgets and staffing. Still, with the lower overhead and higher profit margins of a do-it-yourself business model, you can make more than enough money to live a great life.

Recording and distributing music is easier than it ever has been. There is no longer a need for the "label services" of the past. This business model is much leaner.

These days you can record on your computer, which bypasses traditional recording studios and you can release your music only via the Internet, which bypasses the need for a phonorecord (CD, cassette, 8-track, vinyl, or any other form of physical music distribution), a distribution company, and physical retail outlets.

Thanks to this ease, the financial metrics of your business change. It's cheaper than ever to record music and get it to people. You no longer have to worry about being in "every store" because you can knock out 95 percent of all online distribution, which is where most people buy music now, with just a few key outlets.

Because your financial metrics change, your marketing can change. It's easy (and almost free) to give music away. It's easy (and almost free) to reach your audience directly.

If online marketing is part of your strategy, it can be tracked both accurately and automatically. That means you can focus on what works and drop what doesn't, allowing you to get more for your marketing dollar.

Gone are the days of losing out on sales because you weren't in a record store. Gone are the days of radio being the only way people can sample new music. Gone are the days of having to be vetted by a print magazine for the chance to connect with fans.

As mentioned above, even if you decide to go with a do-it-yourself approach, you'll still need to focus on these three elements of business:

Make the Product

You can't make money if you don't have something to sell.

The product, at its core, is you. Or, more specifically, the way you make people feel. This can be sold through recorded music, live events, or licensing of songs, image, and logos.

Recorded music is the perfect product to illustrate this point. With the exception of a live show, which is not only a means to generate income but also the best promotion method for independent acts, recorded music is the first piece of "you" the majority of fans will purchase.

The popularity of recorded music as a product, plus the fact that "a recording is forever," can put a lot of pressure on independent acts who think anything they release has to be perfect.

French writer François-Marie Arouet said, "*Le mieux est l'ennemi du bien.*"

Loosely translated, this simply means, "Perfect is the enemy of good."

The pursuit of "perfect" will kill a career. Perfect doesn't exist.

This isn't to say that you don't have to do a good job when it comes to creating music. You have to do a *great* job. It's OK to work with the resources you have, though. Many of the most popular recordings in the world, including the most well-known recordings by The Beatles and The Rolling Stones, were recorded on 4-track machines that can't compare to the recording ability of today's free, open-source software on the most basic home computer, tablet, or mobile phone.

Doing the best with what you have to create recordings people want to listen to comes down to two things:

- **A Great Song** – This is the foundation of a good recording, and it happens before you ever step into the studio.

- **A Great Performance** – This is where a great song turns into a legendary recording. When you can give a great performance, you don't need fancy equipment.

People want real. Some of the most popular songs ever recorded have unintelligible lyrics. Some of the most popular recordings of songs have tempo or pitch "problems."

Do music fans complain about tempo and pitch? Not nearly as much as they complain about click tracks and auto-tune. And unintelligible lyrics usually just add to a song's appeal.

The majority of your fans won't care where a song was recorded or who produced it. What people care about is the feeling they get when listening to it.

Remember, this is the "do-it-yourself" recording company business model. The whole point of it is to give you more freedom to play your game. You could record an album in your bathroom and it would be OK.

The *only* thing that matters when it comes to the songs you write, the music you record, or the shows you play is how people feel when they experience them.

Distribute the Product

Regardless of how great your product is, you won't sell a thing if there isn't a way for people to get it.

Thanks to "digital distribution" options such as iTunes or Amazon, this problem is easier to solve than ever. If you're selling a physical product, such as a CD, you can sell it directly to fans during live performances. It's also easy to sell both digital and physical copies of your albums off your own website.

However, what if, for example, you want to go against the grain and release one of your albums exclusively on vinyl?

Do it!

It's important to trust your own decisions, and sometimes, it's best to go with your gut. With the do-it-yourself record label model, you have that option.

But realize that just because you have an option to do something doesn't mean it's a good idea—or that it will be *profitable*.

If you want to release something exclusively in one form or another or in limited release, that's OK. But because you are also a business owner, I encourage you to balance your creativity with more practical considerations.

Sticking with the example, the upside of releasing something on vinyl is that it's cool. You can do a lot with artwork and liner notes. The listening experience is different.

If that's something you want and means a great deal to you, you have every right to go after it.

The downside of releasing something on vinyl is that its appeal is limited; at least as far as music consumption goes. Even if you're able to successfully sell a run of vinyl albums, know that many of the people who buy something on vinyl likely won't be able to play it on anything, because the majority of people listen to music via digital devices, such as iPods and mobile phones.

Does this mean you shouldn't release something on vinyl? Absolutely not. As long as you're able to handle the outcome of limited consumption, there is nothing wrong with doing something like this.

There is almost always a way to balance business and creativity. If, for whatever reason, you want to create a truly exclusive music experience for your fans, know you can find a compromise that will both please you and create ease for your fans. For example, also give those people who purchase your vinyl record a code that allows them to download your music digitally. Not exactly an "exclusive" release, but close.

Market the Product

Nothing sells by itself. To get people to buy something from you, they have to: first, know that it exists, and, second, want it enough to exchange money for it.

This will be your biggest hurdle in having a successful business. With the ease of both recording and distribution, it's the biggest hurdle *any* record label faces.

There are many long-standing beliefs musicians have when it comes to effectively marketing music. One belief is that you must play live shows.

Do you absolutely have to play live shows to be a successful musician?

No. There are plenty of successful musicians who have never played a gig.

But can you get to where *you* want to go without playing a gig? That's what you need to look at before you make a decision as to whether you want to pursue that route.

Every musician is working within his own set of unique circumstances, whether geographic, financial, or something else. Don't let your circumstances stop you from marketing your music both creatively and effectively.

I encourage you to test new marketing techniques and experiment to find successful ways of marketing yourself.

This book is full of music marketing ideas. You can take these ideas as is or modify them to get as creative with your music marketing as you want, tailoring your marketing plan to whatever special needs you have.

Whether you're going against the grain in terms of manufacturing, distributing, or marketing your product, keep in mind that there are good reasons the standard industry practices for these things exist. It's OK for you to break the rules, but it helps to know them first so you can understand exactly what you're getting into and why you're doing it.

IS A RECORD DEAL RIGHT FOR YOU?

Here are things to consider when deciding how to release your music ...

Pick a traditional label model if:

- you want a shot at *big* fame

- money is a secondary goal

- you're OK with letting others drive

... and if you have the following skills:

- you play well with others

- you're willing to compromise

With high risk comes high reward, and that's exactly what you'll get with a traditional label deal. You'll have a lot of overhead (staffing, trucks, warehousing, marketing, recording costs, promotion, etc.), which will require a lot of sales to pay off, but you'll have a big system and a lot of people behind you, helping to get your music out to the world—at least in theory.

The reality of this type of deal is that you've got only a short window to prove yourself. What has traditionally been referred to as "artist development" is all but dead, at least when it comes to labels doing it. If your goal is to be successful with a large record label, it's best that you be fully developed before you do the deal.

Working with a big label, like working with any big company, also requires that you be willing to compromise. These companies have been around for decades, they're well established in how they do business, and they're not going to change for you. For success with this kind of deal, you need to be willing to work *with* the company.

Pick a do-it-yourself model if you're more interested in:

- ownership of your intellectual property

- autonomy

- money over fame

… and if you have the following skills:

- you have the ability to make a decision and stick with it

- you're skilled at finding good people and managing people

Technology is changing quickly. Because of this, there are more and more opportunities for your music.

Ringtones, video games, and smartphone apps were all but a dream in the relatively recent past. What will be the next "dream" that becomes reality—and a new opportunity for you to make money from your music?

Ownership of your intellectual property, whether it's a specific recorded version of a song, the underlying composition of a song, or your name and likeness, is worth something. If you can keep ownership and control of these things, you have a great opportunity to make money.

The Swiss band LiLiPUT (initially known as Kleenex), which broke up in 1983, was offered $50,000 to license its song "Hedi's Head" 20 years after it was first recorded.

That is the power of owning your intellectual property.

The band declined the offer. Had it signed a major record or publishing deal, it might not have had the option to say no.

By the way, the reason LiLiPUT declined was because the company that wanted to use the song was, again, Hummer.

The bottom line is this: If it means a lot to you that your music is available for sale in stores like Wal-Mart or you really want to be on the cover of a magazine like *Rolling Stone*, it will help to have a major label behind you. If you want total control over your image, the songs you play and where you perform, staying independent is the way to go.

Can you have it both ways? Sort of.

As you successfully build your career, you'll find that more and more people want to work with you. The more you have to offer, the better deal you can get for yourself, which will mean more ownership, more control, and more money.

If, in the past, you've been on a major label, it didn't work out like you had hoped, and you were dropped, you can take advantage of your previous exposure by doing something independently.

Sometimes switching up works; sometimes it disconnects your fans.

We've all seen bands that "used to be cool" when they were starting but lost their edge when they moved over to major labels. And fans of major-label-style releases often don't like the less polished, rawer music usually associated with something done independently.

In my opinion, your best option is to think through your career, get very specific about your goals, and pick an approach you'll be OK sticking with. The only reason one model is better than the other will depend on your goals.

Are you OK with turning over ownership of your songs and image?

Are you OK with somebody having a piece of everything, as is the case in 360-type deals?

When digital distribution is the primary way music is being purchased and you can reach almost all digital music buyers simply by going to a company like CD Baby, do you really need distribution help?

What will make you happy? (That's the big one, in my opinion.)

If you want a major label deal because it's what you've always dreamed of, and you understand what you're getting into and what is expected of you, by all means, go for it. Again, play your game and don't apologize.

If we had a crystal ball we'd see some artists who signed major deals but probably would have been better off skipping them. And there are artists who choose the do-it-yourself route who could have been huge had they had major labels behind them.

In the end, you can't get it right and you can't mess it up. There will always be the unknown about any decision you make.

Do what you want with the best information you have at the time, and keep moving forward.

DON'T WAIT TO GET STARTED

No longer is waiting to be "picked" by music business gatekeepers a good excuse for not doing anything. Today, you can do just fine without a record label, broadcast radio stations, print magazines, distribution companies, or record stores getting involved with you at all.

It's nice to be acknowledged by a label or a radio station or the music media, but it's no longer necessary to be able to sell music. People want music that makes them feel good, and none of these things are necessary for that to occur.

Can you handle taking 100 percent responsibility for your success or failure in the music business? If so, you can get started today.

CONCLUSION

Earl Nightingale once said that most people approach life like a man standing in front of a stove who says, "Give me heat and then I'll add wood."

Most artists approach the music business in the same way.

Regardless of the business model you select or whether you want a major label deal, an indie deal, or no deal at all, always remember you must be the one to get the ball rolling. Always.

Be open (and ready) for opportunity, but don't bet your career on a record label fantasy.

Although one person can make a difference in your music career and you never know who this person will be or where she'll show up, nobody is going to care about your music as much as you do. And if you don't care, why should anybody else?

Too often, artists get lost in the fantasy of what could happen in the future—record deals, world tours, hit songs, millions of fans, great press, and radio play. They dream of somebody coming along, championing their music, and pushing them to the next level.

Here's where this gets destructive: While thinking about the future, they neglect (or refuse) to do what is needed in the present.

What's happening in the present isn't always exciting, but if you want to have a better future and be successful in the music business, you *must* invest the time, effort, and money necessary to take care of what is needed now.

That is how you get lucky. Seneca, a first-century Roman philosopher, put it best when he said, "Luck is where the crossroads of opportunity and preparation meet."

Do it now. Do it now. Do it now. The record deal, world tour, hit songs, and everything else will work itself out.

CHAPTER 4:

CLAIM YOUR SPACE

One of the great things about the music business is that there is room for everybody. It doesn't matter if you're a lesbian folksinger, a right-wing songwriter, or a Muslim rapper; there is a place for you. If you really want to be here, space for you to do your thing will appear when you aren't afraid to do it—and you do it well.

Too often, I run into musicians who say things like, "Labels aren't signing anybody who sounds like _____ right now."

Not true. If you're doing something that can't be ignored, which means you're selling music, you'll get signed. (Assuming you want to be signed ...)

There has always been "room for everybody" on a certain level, but the way music was distributed made it impossible to make money if you didn't have some level of mass appeal. When we had to put music in a physical container, such as a vinyl record, a cassette, or a CD, not only did we have to manufacture something, we also had to find a way to get it to the people who wanted it.

Working within the old system, because of the way distribution was, meant you had to have a product that "most people" would like. That meant playing it safe. It meant not rocking the boat. Anything that pushed the limits too much would likely turn people off.

Playing it safe and trying to win over the average person was a good way to succeed with the system we had at the time, when music buyers weren't easy to reach and marketing options were limited. It was the business equivalent of a shotgun—point in the basic direction and hope you hit something.

The problem was that musicians and fans alike never got what they really wanted. Musicians couldn't release their full artistic visions, because they were economically forced to create something "everybody" would buy. People who bought what was released didn't get what they really wanted either, because it was watered down and safe. It was as if the record companies were saying to the fans, "You don't have to love it, just don't hate it enough to turn it off."

Today is different. Thanks to the Internet, distribution is essentially free. There are powerful "promotion outlets" beyond broadcast radio or television stations. It's also easier to connect like-minded people together, whether it's an audience looking for a specific type of music or somebody with music looking for a specific type of audience.

USE A LASER, NOT A WRECKING BALL

Approach your music business like you would if you were running an online dating site.

A website like Match.com has millions of people on it. The owners of this site have made a lot of money being an "everything to everyone" kind of dating experience. The problem is, there is very little room for general sites like this.

That's why "niche" dating sites exist. These sites don't cater to everybody, and because of that, it's easier to reach the people they do cater to. Customers are also willing to pay a premium price to get exactly what they want.

Some of these sites have only a few thousand paying subscribers. For a well-run company, that's enough to make a profit month after month.

Here are some examples of sites that cater to very specific segments of the population:

- DateMyPet.com for cat ladies and the men who love them

- WomenBehindBars.com for guys who are into incarcerated women

- 420dating.com for those looking for a "higher" love

What does this have to do with you and your music? Simply put, broadcast media has become the same way.

At one time, there were three major television networks in the United States. Each had similar content: there were news programs; something for the general adult population, like dramas; and something for kids, like cartoons. There were variety shows, which took the concept of "something for everybody" and put it into a one-hour program.

Today, video content has been set free from the television. It can be distributed in ways much cheaper than the traditional, over-the-air broadcast tower. Receiving equipment isn't limited by the small amount of frequencies it can pick up. It's also much, much cheaper to produce video content to broadcast.

What does this mean?

It means people have options. It means the market has been split from just three segments into thousands. If you count YouTube, it means there are more options than there are people on Earth.

"General interest" content doesn't work on something like YouTube. And because music is now distributed in a similar way, it means that "general interest" content won't work for you either.

Fortunately, this is a great opportunity! It's exactly the reason you should let the world know who you are and not try to hide it. Trying to please everybody pleases nobody.

If you look strictly at numbers, it can be very tempting to play the "just a small percentage" game, where you try to get everybody excited about your music, thinking that simply winning over a small percentage of the general population is all it will take for a song or record to become a hit.

An example of this sort of perspective would sound something like this:

"Well, with over 7,000,000,000 people in the world, we just have to win over 0.000000143 percent of them to sell the 1,000 CDs we just pressed! How hard can that be?"

Harder than you'd think.

Music isn't a one-size-fits-all commodity product like crude oil, soybeans, and pork bellies. It's not sold based on volume, and all music isn't equal to all people, so don't treat it like it is.

If you're willing to work a little, selling 10,000 (or more) copies of an album is completely doable. To make it happen, though, you have to go to the people who like what you're releasing.

This means knowing not only who your audience is, but also knowing as much as you can about them.

Why take time to really get an in-depth knowledge of who your audience is?

Promoting an album can be both time consuming and costly. To save both time and money, it helps to narrow down your audience, give them exactly what they want, and approach them where they are.

YOUR IDEAL CUSTOMER

If you were to open a hamburger stand, what is the one factor that would ensure it would be a success?

Think about it ... The answer probably *isn't* what you think. It's not good customer service, the best beef, a great location, a nice atmosphere, or tasty food (although those things would certainly help).

To be successful in *any* business, whether it be selling hamburgers or selling music, the one thing you will always need is "hungry" customers.

Who is "hungry" for your music?

MUSIC MARKETING SIMPLIFIED

We buy things from people we like. We want to deal with people we can relate to. We want to see a "face" behind the company.

Taking the human element out of business is where most musicians screw up big time. When it comes to marketing, they tend to keep their distance from fans. Doing so makes things impersonal.

For maximum results with your music marketing, people need to feel like they know you, like you, and trust you. Only when these things happen will they spend money with you.

Do not take yourself out of the marketing process by acting "untouchable" or too much like a company. This limits your ability to connect with people in the way that is needed to do business.

You are living the life that most people wish they could. While they're working at a job, you're playing music.

Playing music is fun. Working a job is not fun.

Musicians are fun. Music business executives who wear suits and work at companies are not fun.

In your marketing, just like you do on stage, give people more fun and less business. Make them feel as if they're dealing with you directly, because you're fun. The more people associate you with fun, the better they'll like you and the more they'll buy from you.

FUN WORKS BOTH WAYS

People don't like being sold to. People do like buying things, though — *if* you can make the experience fun.

Not only should your music marketing be fun for your fans, but it should also be fun for you. You got into the music business because playing music is enjoyable, so do what you can to make the marketing aspects of your music business enjoyable as well.

To have more fun with your music marketing, make it more personable. How do you do that? You can start by asking yourself the following questions:

- Who is the guy who buys all your albums?

- Who is the girl dancing in the front at every show you play?

- Who is the Facebook user who always has a comment for whatever you post?

Basically, what you're asking is this:

"Who is a symbolic representation of my ideal fan?"

You are here because of your fans. Without fans, you have nothing. They are the most important part of your music business. Because of this, you need to talk to fans like you would your best friend, a close relative, or a spouse. In other words, like an individual person rather than a nameless, faceless mob.

If you've ever done any public speaking, you're probably familiar with the "trick" of speaking to one person at a time. This helps many speakers get over the nervousness that often comes with speaking to large groups but also deliver a more personal message that each individual can connect with.

When you are marketing yourself and your music, thinking of a single, idealized fan works in a similar way. It will keep you focused on who the real customer is and help you to communicate with fans (and potential fans) more effectively by humanizing them.

Instead of writing songs, recording music, and performing shows for a mass of anonymous faces, you'll start to focus on seeing each fan as an individual. In addition, focusing on the guy who listened to your music on his way to work, who knows every lyric by heart and can't wait until you play his town again, is much more exciting than focusing on a generic demographic, such as "males age 18–34 with a median household income of $35,000."

Always be thinking of an individual in your audience to help you better connect with fans at all levels—from the songs you write to the products you release to where you book shows.

7 TIPS TO BUILD RAPPORT WITH FANS (OR ANYBODY)

People, your fans included, are most receptive to those whom they like, know, and trust. Here are seven tips to help you build rapport with people, so that these things happen:

- **Assume Rapport Is Already There** – Your fans, through your songs and other activities, already feel as if they know you, so when meeting them in person, continue on this path. Skip the awkward, "getting to know you" phase when you're introduced and go straight into talking to people as if you've known them for years.

- **Be Approachable** – Be open. For example, if you're having a conversation and you see a person waiting on the sideline to talk to you, let him or her in. Be confident, yet humble.

- **Listen** – If you can makes fans feel good, they'll do anything for you. Simply listening to fans during interactions with them is a great way to show that you care, build their confidence, and make them feel great about the experience.

- **Be Vulnerable** – Nothing is flawless. Even a slight "damaging admission" when something goes wrong shows you realize and accept imperfection. It will go a long way to building trust with the people you meet.

- **Let People Help You** – People want to be part of what you're doing. If you get an offer from a fan to help you promote a show, work your merch table, or introduce you to someone influential, don't automatically dismiss it. While not every fan (or every offer) will be a good match for you, most people are honest, have good intentions, and really do want to help.

- **Look for Things in Common** – People like those who are like them. Focus on the similarities you have with your fans.

- **Remember Names** – If you're not good at this, figure out a way to get good. Nothing makes people feel more important than being remembered.

"DANCE WITH THE ONE THAT BRUNG YA"

When you have something that is working for you, keep doing it. In the South we have a saying for this: "Dance with the one that brung ya."

For a sports coach, this means to play the players and use the strategies that got you where you are. For a musician, it means that if you're having success with a certain market, don't neglect them.

Abraham Lincoln talked of a similar philosophy at the height of the American Civil War when he said, "It's not best to swap horses when crossing a stream."

Yet this is exactly what many musicians do. They neglect the people (or groups of people) with whom they've had success.

Let's take another look at the career of Martha Wash, the powerful female singer in C+C Music Factory's massive hit "Gonna Make You Sweat (Everybody Dance Now)." Due to her large size, she was left out of the video. She also didn't receive credit for her work in the album's liner notes.

The producers and marketing team behind C+C Music Factory, the ones who thought she was "unmarketable," completely neglected her earlier success. By 1990, Wash had already spent more than a decade as a well-known singer in the gay community. As one half of the duo Two Tons 'o Fun, she was well known as a backup singer for the drag performer and disco star Sylvester. As The Weather Girls, she and Two Tons 'o Fun member Izora Armstead recorded the gay anthem "It's Raining Men."

So where is Martha Wash now?

Today she is as successful as ever, working as an in-demand session vocalist, as well as recording and touring as a solo artist. Her voice is among the most recognized in house music, and her work with acts like Sylvester and Luther Vandross is considered classic, not novelty.

As for her relationship with C+C Music Factory, she successfully sued to receive proper credit and appropriate royalties. Because of her, there is now legislation making vocal credits mandatory on recorded music and music videos.

Martha Wash doesn't try to please the masses or jump on trends. She's focused on her core audience in the gay community, and she's dug in deep. The video for her debut solo single featured her surrounded by half-naked men, she's a top draw at "Pride" events, and she performs at gay clubs throughout the world.

How can you find your own audience so you can do something similar?

START WHERE YOU ARE

If you were to start a new band today, regardless of your experience or past successes in the music business, there would be opportunities to market yourself that you came to the table with, even before sitting down to write a single song or playing one note. These would include people you had a natural advantage of winning over, from communities you're already part of—people you know from work or a religious organization, for example.

Religious-based music is one of the best examples of the power of this concept. If your music is focused around a specific religious philosophy, you will be instantly tapped into an audience of people who will like, or at least appreciate on some level, what you're doing.

There is also a natural advantage to connect with fans based on a shared physical environment or activity in which you both participate, such as a hobby. For example, if you like drinking beer or partying on a beach, there is an opportunity to connect with people who relate to that lifestyle and want to hear you sing songs about it.

When you're a member of a group—whether it be a formal organization, such as a church, or something more loosely knit, such as people who enjoy the beach—you'll have a much easier time connecting to people within that group than somebody from the outside would.

A great example of a type of connection is the one you share with other musicians. As a musician, you have certain things in common with other musicians, so when you meet each other, there is likely instant rapport.

I play guitar. If you were looking for a guitarist for your band, what would the audition look like?

Probably something like this:

1. You give me a list of songs you already know.

2. I learn the songs.

3. I arrive at your rehearsal space with a guitar.

4. We tune up.

5. We play the songs.

That's the ritual of trying out for a band. It's the way you see if somebody fits. There is a very specific communication style (and language) that is used. You don't have to explain it to me, because I already know.

Every group—whether it's formal, like a church congregation, or informal, such as musicians—has its own version of this. If you're tapped into how the group thinks and feels, you'll be successful with them.

THE "SECRET CODE" OF FANS

Once you've established who your ideal fans are, it's easy to get an idea of the way they think and communicate with one another simply by observing them. Thanks to the Internet, this process is faster and easier than ever.

Even though you may personally be part of the community you are marketing to, there may be certain values, beliefs, and desires of your fan base that you are not 100 percent tapped into.

For example, the majority of your fans might be blue-collar workers who live in the same city you do, come to the bars you play, and root for the same sports teams you do, but you might not be able to relate to them fully because you come from a wealthy family and have never had a 9-to-5 job.

Or maybe you're *not* part of the community you're marketing to at all! That happens with songwriters all the time …

For example, the majority of your fans may be teenage girls who yearn to meet a boy and be in a romantic relationship, but you might not be able to relate because you're a guy and your "first love" was years ago.

Either way, you need to tap into the minds of your fans to find out how they think and feel!

Sites like Twitter, Facebook, and Amazon allow you to "enter the conversation" fans (and potential fans) are already having with one another. You can watch their interactions, find out what they like (and don't like) about things, and learn what gets them excited.

It's easy to sell music (or other merchandise) and get people to shows when you know what people will pay money for. This isn't manipulation, nor will it take you away from your natural creative process; it's simply providing people with exactly what they want. This will make your marketing process easier, save you time, and keep you on fans' minds, since you are fulfilling an emotional need they are looking to fill.

LET YOUR FREAK FLAG FLY

Don't follow somebody else's formula. Instead, "fly your flag" and be proud of it.

You've probably met somebody who was completely left-of-center yet was respected by everybody, because he acted in such a way that there was no question about his authenticity. That's the kind of person who is often successful in the music business.

Examples of artists with this quality:

- Pete Burns

- Lady Gaga

- Liberace

- Michael Jackson

- Axl Rose

- David Allan Coe

This is more than wearing a certain type of clothing, flaunting your sexuality, or being vulgar (although these things can be part of it). It's not about what you do, but how you do it.

When it comes to your professional persona, be who you are, but do it bigger and bolder. The most memorable artists don't hold back.

If everybody else seems to think "zig" and you think "zag," embrace it.

Why? Because, regardless of who you are and whatever you're doing, there will be people who relate to you. Authenticity is the glue of connection. It will allow you to connect with fans in such a way that they'll not only want to buy everything you come out with, but they'll happily pay a premium price. They'll do so because they appreciate that you have the guts to say what they're thinking and act like they'd like to act but, for whatever reason, feel they can't.

When it comes to your music career, don't wimp out and do things halfway. Be bold in your actions, and, if you do something that agitates some people or makes them uncomfortable, be bold in how you handle the blowback.

WATCH FOR PATTERNS

There are times when we do something that others positively relate to in a way we would never have expected. When that happens, go with it.

For example, if you're in a band and bikers start showing up to your gigs, embrace it. If lesbians start showing up to your gigs, embrace it. If burnouts start showing up to your gigs, embrace it. Don't leave money on the table.

Journalist Malcolm Gladwell gave a great non-music example of this in his book *The Tipping Point*.

According to the book, in 1994, sales of Hush Puppies shoes were down to 30,000 pairs a year, and its parent company, Wolverine Worldwide, was considering phasing out the brand. The next year, Hush Puppies suddenly became hip in the clubs and bars of downtown Manhattan. That fall, fashion designers John Bartlett, Anna Sui, and, Joel Fitzpatrick began featuring them in their collections. Thanks to word of mouth and famous customers like Jim Carrey, David Bowie, and Tom Hanks, 430,000 pairs of the shoes were sold, with four times that the following year.

Hush Puppies weren't designed to be hip; they were designed to be comfortable. They're the kind of shoes your grandfather wears. Still, when things started taking off with the hipster population, Wolverine didn't stop it.

The majority of the time, an unintended audience is a blessing. If one happens to find you and likes the music that you're making, go with it.

Don't ignore new opportunities that pop up. Even if they're from people who don't look like your core audience, those opportunities are still worth money.

ALIENATE SOME PEOPLE

Too often, musicians play it safe for fear of alienating people. A far bigger problem, which happens when you play it safe, is that you'll be ignored.

By alienating some people, you will connect more deeply with others.

You don't have to be liked by everybody to be successful. Just a small number of people who really love you is all it takes to have a great career.

People who are hated by some and loved by just as many:

- Donald Trump

- Rush Limbaugh

- Michael Moore

- Al Gore

- Sarah Palin

- Barack Obama

- George W. Bush

- Simon Cowell

The best *music* examples of this are from acts that have specific religious or political philosophies. Any Christian act is going to alienate those who aren't Christians, at least on some level, but those who *are* Christian are going to buy in even more.

Think about it: if you're Christian, you'd much rather hear "Jesus is Lord" than something about a "higher power," because "Jesus is Lord" is a sentiment you can relate to. Because of this, an act that gives specific references to Jesus is going to connect with Christians in a very powerful way.

If you're a Christian act, who cares if some people are offended or turned off by Jesus? You're a Christian act! Focus on the Christians. Nobody else cares about you, so don't worry about them.

The same thing applies to *any* act. Embrace polarization. Anything else falls in the middle—and the middle is forgettable by everybody.

EMBRACE THE SLOW BURN

When you have a CD that hits really big and is available everywhere, it's now considered a "commodity." With sales outlets (both online and offline) all selling the same CD, the most common way they compete for sales is to lower the price.

For example, if your album sells for $9.99 on iTunes, Google, which wants to compete with iTunes, might drop the price to $3.99. Amazon, if it wants to get in, might drop the price even more. In 2011, Amazon's servers crashed when they sold Lady Gaga's entire *Born This Way* album for only $0.99.

A price war among the big digital music outlets can certainly sell a lot of albums, but consider the potential downsides.

For one, as mentioned, because everybody is basically selling the exact same commodity with the exact same ease of purchase and speed of delivery, and because fewer and fewer music buyers today are considered brand loyal, the only sure way to compete for sales is price. This means less and less money is being made on big releases.

In addition, with so many people buying at once, there is a "churn and burn" element with big releases. Buyers are moving on to the next big thing more quickly than ever.

Compare that with a "slow-burn" release, where the promotion of an album can last months (and sometimes years), which is what so many independent artists, especially those in niche markets, choose instead.

When you're not everywhere at once, you can charge a higher price for your product, as it's harder to come by. In addition, because there will be fewer impulse buys, the price will stay higher for a longer period of time. Because fewer buyers will be selling your product on the used market, those who do, due to lack of supply, will be able to get higher prices. This will help keep perceived value of your products high, even on sites like eBay or the used section on Amazon.

The best aspect of a slow-burn product has less to do with pricing and more to do with how the album is valued. More often than not, people who buy via a slow-burn release are more loyal than consumers who simply follow trends. Not only will they enjoy that they got in on buying something exclusive, they'll be more likely to spread the word about the purchase and about how much they like your music. This helps build your relationships with fans and encourages them to buy more products, come to more shows, and continue to tell more people about what you're doing.

With a slow-burn release, you give quality over quantity. This can lead to not only a long career, but more money when all is said and done.

Don't worry if you don't sell millions of records right away. You can do just as well in the long run, even if you don't sell that many.

You don't need a massive fan base to make enough money for a very nice lifestyle. You need only a core group of dedicated fans who are willing to stick with you and buy from you again and again.

Most independent releases are of the "slow-burn" variety, whether planned or not. This is simply because it's very difficult to be everywhere at once. Still, you can have even more success using this technique by being deliberate about continuing to push your album over an extended period of time.

Just as the "slow burn" applies to music you release, it also applies to your career in general. This is perhaps the most important aspect to internalize when it comes to claiming your space within the music industry.

Any artist, regardless of how good you are, will have ups and downs in your career if you stick it out long enough. Most artists are fine at the beginning of their careers, when they have nowhere to go but up. But what happens when they finally "make it" and have to deal with drops in popularity?

Perhaps this is where the real work happens, because many acts fade away shortly after hitting it big. They had success, at least for a time, but couldn't keep it up.

How can you keep up success? Embrace the slow burn.

Your career will be a series of peaks and valleys. Often, some of the biggest valleys are those that happen after your highest peaks. The opposite is also true.

Knowing this, if you keep showing up and claiming your space, you'll be fine.

FLASH IN THE PAN

Popular music styles come and go. Some hit once, never to be heard from again, while others disappear only temporarily, returning to be permanently cemented among the most successful genres of music.

A great example of this happening to an entire style of music is the genre most people refer to as "hair metal."

In the late 1980s, hair metal (also known as glam rock) was huge. Around that time, Motley Crue singer Vince Neil appeared on the cover of *Musician Magazine*, lighting a cigar with a $100 bill. The headline story talked about a multimillion-dollar advance the group had just secured.

Within a couple of years, the entire genre seemed to have vanished.

Lots of hair metal acts tried to change things up. Some, like Motley Crue, went harder. Many tried a grunge-like sound, to compete with industry darlings like Nirvana and Pearl Jam.

But hair metal didn't die; it only experienced a brief pause. Although it was no longer on mainstream radio or MTV, it was still out there.

Those who stuck with the formula they'd had success with found that people *were* interested. The genre was still popular in certain parts of the United States, and, although acts weren't selling as many records as they had at one time, there was enough interest in them that they were able to continue touring.

People *were* interested. Independent labels like CMC International were a haven for hair metal acts when major labels were focusing on grunge and alternative rock acts.

Eventually, enough time passed to when hair metal was cool again. People longed for the novelty, the big shows, and the party atmosphere these acts provided. The tours got bigger and bigger.

Today, many hair metal acts are among the most successful touring acts on the road.

This is the slow burn in action. Sometimes it will burn a little brighter than others, but it will never go out completely.

Keep showing up and doing your work.

9 WAYS TO KEEP YOUR CAREER MOVING FORWARD

It's easy to get lost in both the highs and lows of a music career. When things are going well, it can be dangerous to think it will never end, but even more dangerous to be so paranoid about it ending that you stop taking chances. And when things *aren't* going well, it can be easy to focus on the negative and forget the good work you are doing.

Here are nine strategies to help you claim your space in the music business and keep your career moving forward.

- **Don't Worry About Other People** – Do what you do and forget what everybody else is doing. Music centers like Nashville, New York, and LA are full of the best musicians and songwriters in the world, and they can be extremely intimidating if you start to compare yourself to them.

  Again, sometimes not knowing everything is a great advantage.

- **Focus on the Outcome** – If you know what you want to happen, go for it. Don't worry about every single detail. Most won't matter anyway, since you really have no idea what you're getting into until you jump in 100 percent.

Clarity is the most important thing needed to make anything happen. When you're clear on why you want something, the strength and perseverance you need in order to make it happen will come through.

When your "why" is big enough, you're ready to take on anything.

- **If It Works, Keep Doing It!** – When you find a music marketing strategy (or anything else) that works for you, keep at it consistently. If it works a little, it will usually work a lot with increased effort.

- **Avoid the Cave** – When you're not in the process of releasing something or touring, don't hide out. People have short attention spans, so do what you can to consistently be creating, releasing, and promoting products.

  If you've just come off a tour and you're exhausted, it's fine to take a little break, but don't totally disappear. Do something to keep fans engaged, whether it be releasing previously recorded material, playing a benefit show, or interacting online.

- **Don't Follow Trends** – Trends come and go. Forget that. If what you're doing isn't hot right now, but it works for you, keep at it anyway. This not only applies to the music you play, but also everything else about your career.

  For example, if the majority of people are saying a certain social media site is dead, but it works for you, keep at it until it doesn't work for you. You're going for results, not trying to impress people by being on top of the latest social media trend.

- **Don't Look Down** – Focus on the job that needs to be done. Don't "look down" or obsess about the things that can go wrong.

This is the music business. There are plenty of things that can go wrong. Getting caught up in the distraction of worrying about the potential of negative things happening is usually far more dangerous than any of the negative things actually happening.

- **See Opportunities** – Opportunities to speak to your audience, get publicity, connect with somebody important, make money, or otherwise grow your music business are all around you. Be on the lookout for them.

If you're in an airport, especially in Nashville, LA, or NYC, and you see a guy carrying a guitar, that's an opportunity for you to make a connection. If you're on an airplane and you don't have a copy of your music to give to somebody you meet, you're missing an opportunity.

- **Follow Opportunities** – Make things happen. Nothing happens without action.

This means walking up to somebody and introducing yourself, making a phone call, or sending a demo. Without follow-up, nothing happens.

- **Know When You're Getting Lucky** – Mark Twain once said, "I was seldom able to see an opportunity until it had ceased to be one." How many overnight sensations, such as the ones on YouTube or *American Idol*, could say the same thing? Most of them.

When something good happens to you, do what you can to keep the momentum going. Even the biggest hit doesn't last forever.

CONCLUSION

There are people who want to hear from you, but you're going to have to find them, because they're too busy and inundated with noise to find you. Do it.

Today, because of the way music is recorded and distributed, there is more room in this business than ever. When you show up ready to do the work, you'll find there is room for you!

CHAPTER 5:

CONNECT WITH YOUR AUDIENCE

True connection, like the one you want with your fans, can best be summed up with this quote by Ernest Hemingway:

"When people talk, listen completely. Most people never listen."

That is the secret to the music business. It's not about songs, musicianship, or anything else as much as it is making people feel like they've been heard. This is done by giving the people in your audience a voice, saying the things they can't, and saying the things they feel … and that starts by listening to their needs.

Empathy is the capacity to recognize feelings that are being experienced by another. This is your *number-one* music marketing skill.

If you can master empathy, you can master the music business. When you understand what people really mean when they speak, why they go to shows, and what gets them to take action, you can write your own ticket.

If you take away one thing from this book, take away this:

Let your audience be the star.

You may be the one on stage, but a live performance is never about you.

Never. It's always about your audience. More specifically, how it makes them feel.

If you can make people feel good, you can get anything you want in this business.

EMPATHY – AN ESSENTIAL (AND PROFITABLE) SKILL

The ability to see things through the eyes of another person is one of the most valuable "music business" skills you can have. Only when you really understand people and where they are coming from can you create an experience or product that directly meets their needs.

If you've ever heard a song and thought, "That song is about me!! I could have written that," you've experienced the connecting power of empathy.

While it is not possible to completely understand where somebody is coming from without actually being that person, the skill of empathy can be developed to a point where you are very, very close. Here are four ways you can do that:

- **Withhold Judgement** – Set aside your beliefs, baggage and personal agenda. There are 7,000,000,000 people in the world and 7,000,000,000 ways to live. We all grow up having different experiences that influence how we feel and act. Is one better than another? Maybe … but if you want to develop and showcase your empathy, don't go there.

- **Listen** – One of the cruelest things you can do to another person is to ignore them. On the flip side, listening to what somebody has to say is one of the most effective ways to make him feel cared for and build both trust and connection. This is especially powerful when you listen while withholding judgement.

- **Ask Questions** – There is a reason for everything, and questions allow you to find out why people act or think the way they do. Questions show you are interested in somebody and give you an opportunity to listen to them, which will build connection even more.

- **Find Common Ground** – We like people who are similar to us. This is why the majority of people segregate themselves based on race, social or economic status, gender, religion, or political belief. You can take advantage of the human preference for this by connecting on common issues and feelings.

One of the best things a musician can do to develop his career and sell more music is to work at a record store. There is no better way to learn why people are buying music and what record labels have to do in order to make this happen.

The changing face of the business is making record store jobs scarce, but if you want to learn firsthand why people are consuming music and how they're doing it, there are still plenty of opportunities that will help you. For example:

- **Wedding DJ** – If you want to learn what gets people out of their seats and onto the dance floor, there is no better job than a wedding DJ. Weddings are awkward, long, and self-indulgent. People don't want to be there. People are uncomfortable, having to talk to people they don't know or don't like. If you can find a way to motivate this crowd, motivating the music fans you normally deal with will be a breeze.

- **Street Musician** – People on the street are busy. They're usually going somewhere. What gets them to put whatever they're doing on hold, stop, and enjoy music? That's what you'll learn when you perform on the street.

- **Party Band** – Similar to a wedding DJ, performing with a "party band" will get you in front of a general audience of people and allow you to see what motivates them.

Need a day job? Are you in a place that has no "music industry" jobs, but you're looking for something that will help you develop skills you can use to further your music career?

If you're interested in getting to the heart of what gets people to buy anything and to understand people better in general, the following opportunities will help you get good at sizing people up quickly, having an answer to any objection they have, and closing deals:

- **Telephone Sales** – Yes, telemarketing. It's not a glamorous job, but any kind of telephone sales, especially the kind where you're calling people (instead of having them call you), will build your communication and sales skills like no other job out there. Want to increase your ability to connect and close deals with booking agents, club owners, and other music industry people who you call on the phone? This is the way to do it!

- **Door-to-Door Sales** – Nothing builds up your tolerance for rejection more than having to knock on the doors of people who aren't expecting you, are skeptical of you, and weren't in the market for what you're selling. Like a job in telephone sales, selling door to door will help you develop both communication and closing skills. And you'll get really good at dealing with rejection in an effective way, since you can't just disappear by hanging up on somebody when things go wrong.

- **Street Sales** – If you've ever been to Las Vegas, you'll see these guys everywhere. Whether it's selling a free presentation to talk about timeshare properties or a "Free Personality Test" by the Church of Scientology, the skills of communication and sales that you develop from doing a cold approach on the street will come in handy for your music business career.

It sounds crazy for a musician to take any of these non-music related sales jobs, doesn't it?

It's not. Here's why …

A basic level sales job will help you to get good at:

- Talking

- Dealing with Rejection

- Overcoming Objections

- Grabbing Attention

- Closing the Sale

Every single one of these things is a skill that will help you to further your music business.

In addition, these jobs will give you the opportunity to connect with hundreds (and even thousands) of people. This will help you get to know why they think, feel, and act the way they do. You'll learn what gets people to take action and buy.

When you really understand people, you can offer them exactly what they're asking for. When this happens, they'll search you out, tell friends, and pay a premium price.

TWO ACTS, TWO OUTCOMES

I once worked with a management company that handled the career of an artist who had, at the time, sold about 10,000,000 records. He was well known but had lost some heat and wasn't as popular as he had been. His latest album had been considered a flop.

By "considered a flop," I mean that his most recent album wasn't even Gold (500,000 copies sold). The sales he did have were great by most standards, but when compared to his past Platinum (1,000,000 copies sold) and Multi-Platinum albums, a lot of people thought he had peaked and was going downhill.

His record deal ended. Word on the street was that he was dropped, although if you ask him, he'd argue that he left.

And he very well may have left, because the week after his contract was terminated, he was signed to an even *bigger* label—and was back in business once again.

I asked the head manager how he'd done it. He told me, "He's still relevant and he's still making money. He has 80,000 people *paying* to be in his fan club."

And he's *still* relevant. Today, over a decade later, he's doing as well as ever.

Around the same time, I saw an independent act doing a showcase in Las Vegas. There was a huge buzz around them, mainly because they had been very successful giving away free music online, which was considered a bold move at the time. Even before they walked on stage, almost everybody there had heard them already.

They signed a major-label deal that year. It made sense, because millions of people had downloaded their music and had already been exposed to them. They had a proven product that had already been "tested" in the real world. Who wouldn't want the entire album?

The album was released. The first-week sales were under 200 copies.

By the way, this happens more often than you'd think. There are plenty of major-label releases, many from well-known artists, that never sell more than 10,000 copies.

Still, fewer than 200 copies for a band with so much buzz is almost unbelievable.

So what happened?

Most likely, the reason was that few of those people who had previously downloaded the band's music were told there was a new album being released. They simply didn't know it existed.

A simple email to even a portion of the act's fans would have likely changed the outcome of how successful their album was.

The ability to connect with your fans is worth more than any heat you have (or don't).

Don't expect people to know what you're doing. When you're releasing something new, or when you're playing a show, you must tell them.

IF A TREE FALLS AND NOBODY IS AROUND TO HEAR IT ...

Want to sell tickets to a show? Albums? The first step is letting people know you're doing it.

If nobody knows what's happening, nobody will take action. It doesn't matter who you're working with or how good the product is. You could put together a show with the most popular band ever—for example, Abba. To better your odds of selling tickets, you could add Lady Gaga, Led Zeppelin, and U2 to the bill. If nobody knows there is an option to buy tickets, though, none of this matters.

If you want to sell something, you have to let people know you have something for sale. Don't expect people to come to you with a pocket full of money and beg to give it to you.

The first act I mentioned had a list of 80,000 *paying* customers via a fan club. These were people who not only "raised their hands" to say they were interested, but they had also come forward with their money and contact information. They *wanted* to be contacted with information about him and his career.

The second act I mentioned had a lot of people who were curious about them and had downloaded free music, but they had failed to get contact information from them. Once these people hit the site and downloaded the music, they were gone, without any way to follow up with them.

Were these people listening to and enjoying the free music? Chances are, with millions of songs downloaded, a lot of them were. Would some of them have purchased a full album, if given the chance? Yes!

They were never given that chance, though.

"THOSE GUYS ARE STILL AROUND?"

Have you ever looked up a band you liked only to find out they have a new album available that you hadn't previously heard anything about? It happens all the time.

Eighty-four percent of people don't know when their favorite band has released a new album.

The people who like your music are busy. They're doing the things people do—refinancing mortgages, trying to get promoted at work, or worrying about whether they'll look good for their high school reunion. While they like your music, it's not their primary focus.

However, they will be interested *if* you let them know about it.

Keeping in touch with your fans and letting them know you have new music (or are playing shows near them) is easier than ever!

The current model, which doesn't apply to traditional media, such as newspapers and television, but applies to social media and almost everything being done online, looks like this:

Musician ⇨ Fan

It also looks like this …

Fan ⇨ Musician

Either way, it's just you and your fans. There is no middleman. You can go straight to them, and they can come straight to you.

No longer do you have to worry about "filters," such as editors, reporters, producers, A&R people, or record distribution companies. Today, it's just you, the message you want to send, and the fan.

Beyond the ability to talk directly with fans, no longer are you constricted by the limited space, frequency, or distribution of traditional media (broadcast radio, print magazines, and television). Today, you have almost unlimited space for your message, distribution is far reaching, and you can send as many messages as you want. Plus, all of this is cheap, easy, and instant.

Most of the time, this type of connection and lack of filters is great. For example, if you just recorded a great acoustic version of your biggest hit and want to either give it away or sell it to a worldwide audience, you can make that happen within about an hour.

The downside is, if you act like an idiot, such as posting photos of yourself dressed in black face or smoking meth, there is nothing in place to keep you from negatively affecting your career.

You must think about this. You have no idea who is "listening" to your Twitter messages, Facebook updates, photos you post, or anything else you put up.

This sounds like common sense, but it's very easy to overlook when you're up late at night or you're tired or you're pissed off or you're thinking that just because you're in your living room with a few friends, what you're putting online (or elsewhere) doesn't matter.

On the Internet, everybody is watching. Always. And once it's out, it's there forever. There is no "undo" button.

OWN THE MEDIA

Whether you want to release music on your own or via a record company, the ability to successfully connect with fans will help you more than anything else. That's because music is subjective, and anything subjective is risky. Being able to communicate with an already existing audience lessens that risk.

This is why an artist who just got dropped from his label can get another record deal within a week.

But not all ways you connect with fans are equal … Having 80,000 followers on Twitter is great, but not nearly as good as having 80,000 people in a fan club that you can connect with via postal mail or phone. And 80,000 people *paying* to be in your fan club is even better, because it shows they think you're good enough to spend money on!

To really take advantage of the power of connecting with your audience, it's important that you're able to keep in touch with them independently of your relationship with a single company, website, or social media tool. You don't want your ability to communicate with fans to be controlled by a company that might go out of business.

Don't think it will happen? Think again. It's happening daily.

Websites like MP3.com and IUMA, which were huge players in the music business at one time, no longer exist. And almost nobody cares about Myspace anymore, so even if you could post a message there, it wouldn't get read.

Twitter accounts can be banned. The same goes for LinkedIn, Facebook, and any other social media site.

When you keep your own list, whether it be via postal mail, email, or phone, you open yourself up to a wide variety of communication options.

Own your ability to connect with your audience.

Working with a third-party company to reach your fans is fine as long as you're able to export fan contact information and use it somewhere else. Proprietary information, such as a Twitter username, is great to have, but if you can use it only on Twitter, and Twitter goes out of business or bans you, it's worthless.

Here is the contact information you want to get from your fans:

- Full Name

- Postal Address

- Email Address

- Phone Number

Having this will allow you to use postal mail, any email marketing service, or any telephone marketing service.

You may think, "I don't need a phone number, because we never call our fans."

Don't let that stop you from asking for it. You might not call (or text) your fans now, but technology is changing, and, should you want to start doing this in the future, you don't want lack of contact information holding you back.

In short, it's nice to have options, and getting complete contact information gives you options.

THE POWER OF ONE

Building your fan base one person at a time doesn't mean you play a show for 100 people and win over only one of them. It doesn't mean you have to personally talk to everybody in the club where you're playing, although that wouldn't be a bad idea.

Building your fan base one person at a time simply means that you treat your fans as individuals rather than a nameless, faceless mob of well-wishers. You see the humanity behind each person as an individual, recognizing that he has unique feelings that need to be addressed in order for him to support you.

A WORD ON FAN RELATIONSHIPS

Fans love being able to hear from you directly, because it's personal. It's no different from the kind of contact they get from the most influential people in their lives, such as parents and friends, and because of this, they'll be more likely to associate you with relationships of this nature.

I was at a "meet and greet" event once in a small, very intimate recording studio. The artist was late, so the label representative grabbed a mic and, in an effort to keep people entertained, started asking people questions about what type of music they listened to and the new artists they liked.

I remember one woman very vividly, because she kept talking like she knew all of the artists being mentioned on a personal level.

"He's such a jokester," she would say. Or, "He's always been a mama's boy."

I talked to her after the event. How did she know all these people?

She *didn't*. But she thought she did because she was interacting with them on Twitter and Facebook as well as similar "meet and greet" events, such as the one we were attending together.

That is the power of "direct-to-fan" contact. If you do it right, people on the receiving end will feel like they know you.

There is a downside to this, though.

As you start to do what I've described in this book regarding building and strengthening relationships with fans, you'll soon run into the problem of "relationship management." If you've been at this a while, you may already be there.

Simply put, how do you maintain relationships with a large number of people?

Before I go any further, realize that there are limits on how many people we can have "quality" relationships with, not only because of time and physical limitations, but because of how our brains work.

British anthropologist Robin Dunbar studied human interaction and developed "Dunbar's Number," which suggests a limit to the number of people with whom one can maintain stable social relationships. These are relationships in which an individual knows who each person is and how each person relates to every other person. The commonly used value is 150.

And that's on the high end!

The number gets to 150 only for communities with a very high incentive to remain together. Plus, for a group of this size to remain cohesive, Dunbar speculated that as much as 42 percent of the group's time would have to be devoted to social grooming.

Don't expect to know everything about each person you come in contact with. You can't be everyone's best friend.

Don't be fooled by all the social media "experts" who appear to be attached to computers or mobile devices 24/7. Even if you were to do this, if you're promoting your music like you should, you'll have way too many fans to respond to every email personally, keep track of every conversation on Facebook, and otherwise "be everywhere."

It will be much better for you to pick one form of communication and do it effectively. I suggest Twitter, since messages are limited to 140 characters. It will allow you to communicate personally, but nobody on the receiving end of your message will be offended by the brevity, because all messages on Twitter are limited.

Pick a time to respond to messages you get, do it, and then let it go. Being tied down to a computer or mobile phone is keeping you from fully experiencing other elements of your day, as well as keeping the people who really care, the ones who got off the social media stuff to actually interact with you in person, from having their full experience.

Trying to be everywhere, when it's impossible to do so, will only leave you worn out and the people you "interact" with pissed off.

As you get to know your fans better and better, it will make your communication much more effective. You'll have quality over quantity, making people feel as if you're "looking right at them" with a personal message, as opposed to what almost every other band is doing, which is just making noise.

You are in charge. Just because everybody else is doing it doesn't mean it's a good idea. Focus on the relationships that count and being "successful, yet approachable" while avoiding the time-suck of busywork.

WAYS TO ENGAGE FANS USING SOCIAL MEDIA

If you've ever wondered why disco music was so popular, one of the reasons is that it enabled an audience, by dressing up and dancing, to become part of the show. Rap music, with call and response style vocals, is popular for the same reason.

Social media outlets, such as Facebook and Twitter, have the same ability. A one-way broadcast message sent via social media can easily turn into a two-way conversation. Taking advantage of this is something that will not only help you spread the word about your music but also allow you to form strong and lasting relationships with your audience.

Here are five easy options for how to do it:

1. **Ask Two-Option Questions** – This is the easiest way to get a response from people. It doesn't take much time or thought for somebody to decide on one of two options and type a single-word answer. These questions also have a very high interaction and discussion rate due to their polarizing nature.

   There are three main types of two-option questions that I suggest:

   - *yes/no* questions
   - *this/that* questions
   - *true/false* questions

   Examples of *yes/no* questions:

   "Should we record an album of all cover songs?"

   "Is the Pope Polish?"

   "Should I grow a beard?"

   Examples of *this/that* questions:

   "Which of these album covers do you like better?"

   "Coke or Pepsi?"

   "David Lee Roth or Sammy Hagar?"

   NOTE: This/that questions are a great way to "test market" things before you actually commit to them. For example, posting two mock-ups of album covers and letting people pick the one they like best will help you have more success when you release your album.

   Examples of *true/false* questions:

   "Centipedes have one hundred legs. – True or False?"

   "Gravity is weaker in North America than in Europe. – True or False?"

   "One of the Bond Girls was born a man! – True or False?"

NOTE: Some of the examples above have nothing to do with music. That's OK. You are trying to build a multifaceted relationship with your fans, and non-music questions will help to do that.

2. **Ask Open-Ended Questions** – Make it easy for the discussion to flow. You're looking for passionate answers from people that will start spinoff discussions. This is where the power of social media really takes off.

   Examples of open-ended questions:

   "What was the first album you ever purchased?"

   "We are going to release a cover album. Any suggestions for songs to record?"

   "What is your favorite song from the 1980s?"

   "How do you find out about new music?"

   "What's the last album you purchased?"

3. **Polls** – A poll-style question is great because it lets your audience get involved in an easy way (selecting from a choice of provided answers) as well as gives you a specific and measurable way to quantify how people feel about something.

   Example of a poll:

   "We want to add a cover song to our set. Which of these do you like best?"

   a. Stigmata – Danzig

   b. Shake Your Love – Debbie Gibson

   c. Abracadabra – Steve Miller Band

   d. Mr. Tambourine Man – The Byrds

4. **Caption Contests** – To maximize interest from a variety of people on Twitter, Facebook, or any other social media outlet,

you'll need to communicate in a variety of ways, including, text, photo, audio, and video.

A caption contest, in which your audience suggests captions for the photos you post, is the perfect way to encourage interaction.

How to do it: Simply post an interesting or funny photo with the description, "Caption this photo!" If you need help picking a winner, use a poll-style question to let your audience decide.

5. **Giveaways** – Everybody likes a giveaway, especially when it's from their favorite musician.

Examples of giveaways:

"AIR GUITAR CONTEST!! First person to upload a video of himself (or herself) playing air guitar to (INSERT SONG HERE) to YouTube gets a free T-shirt."

"First five people to respond to this message get an autographed 'lyric napkin' with lyrics from a song off my new album, (INSERT ALBUM NAME HERE)."

"First ten people to write (INSERT BAND NAME) on a piece of paper, take a photo of themselves, and upload it to Facebook win a copy of my new album, (INSERT ALBUM NAME HERE). NOTE: Be sure to tag me!"

13 TIPS FOR SOCIAL MEDIA SUCCESS

Not all use of social media is equal. Like music video in the 1980s, it has boosted some acts and destroyed others.

Most of what you see being done with social media is a waste of time. The majority of people are thinking very short term, and, if you want success, you've got to think bigger than that. This is not a "get rich quick" opportunity for you to get some quick publicity and a few extra fans; it's a long-term strategy that will allow you to connect to fans in a way never before possible, and you need a plan if you want to succeed with that.

When you post, think about the big picture. This means keeping your message at the forefront of *all* your communication. This isn't the place to talk about everything under the sun or, even worse, air grievances. Your job with social media is to assist your music business, so be focused on that.

Also keep in mind that part of the big picture is listening. The true power of social media isn't that you're able to blast your message at very little cost; it's that everybody can participate in the conversation. Being open to this will draw people in and make what you say on social media even more effective.

When posting anything online ...

- **Speak to an Individual** – Remember, although your messages are going out to hundreds, thousands, or even tens of thousands of people, each will be read by just one person. Whether you're writing an email to your mailing list, posting something on Facebook, or updating your status on Twitter, use the same language you'd use as if you were talking to somebody one on one.

  DO THIS: "I hope to see you at the show tonight!"

  DON'T DO THIS: "I hope to see all my fans at the show tonight!"

  Using the word "you" makes people feel included and recognizes that they are individuals, not a nameless, faceless mob that is part of your marketing strategy.

- **Keep It Short** – Be brief and get to the point.

- **Mix It Up** – Different people prefer different types of content. To connect with as many people as possible, alternate your communication style between photos, audio, videos and text messages.

- **Be Human** – People are looking to connect with something real. Being too polished can actually hurt what you're trying to do, so don't worry about being perfect in your communication.

- **Recognize Specific Fans** – If you have fans who are doing something above and beyond normal, recognize them.

- **Target Via Location** – Filter location-specific messages, such as gigs and record store performances, so that people too far away to attend won't be bothered.

- **Be Timely** – One of the best things about social media is that it's instant. Take advantage of this by asking questions about current hot topics and responding to people as quickly as possible.

- **Push the Edge** – You're a musician. Don't be afraid to piss some people off.

- **Make Them Shine** – When you make others look good, they'll make you look good. Don't hog all the attention. Link to others, ask people questions about themselves, and let them have the spotlight from time to time.

- **Ask for Something** – Don't just talk, listen. Whether you need recommendations for a new guitar or help finding a good Mexican restaurant in Chunky, Mississippi, your social media network can help.

- **Call to Action** – If you want people to ask something, ask for it.

- **Tag People (When Possible)** – If you're posting photos of people, tag them to bring them into the conversation.

- **Keep the Momentum Going** – Don't do a "hit and run." When the conversation starts to move, jump in and keep it going.

SOCIAL MEDIA RULES FOR YOU AND YOUR TEAM

On July 20, 2012, a gunman, dressed in tactical clothing, set off tear gas grenades and shot into the audience during a midnight screening at the Century movie theater in Aurora, Colorado, using multiple firearms. He killed twelve people and injured fifty-eight others.

A few hours later, the following message came through on a Twitter account belonging to the National Rifle Association …

"Good morning, shooters. Happy Friday! Weekend plans?"

Clothing retailer Celeb Boutique had a similar screw-up …

"#Aurora is trending, clearly about our Kim K inspired #Aurora dress," followed by an emoticon wink and a link to a product page.

Both messages were posted several hours after the shootings, well after Twitter was buzzing with talk about what had happened. It's hard to believe that an employee of the largest gun advocacy organization in the country and an outsourced social media team, which obviously knew that "#Aurora" was trending, could miss it.

But they did. And they made the organizations they were working for look like idiots.

Keep your social media in-house, with people like you, who have skin in the game. In addition, if a message isn't coming directly from you, let people know.

Emily White, co-founder of the NYC-based talent management company Whitesmith Entertainment, suggests tagging Twitter messages that don't come directly from you, so people know the difference. For example, if your band is called ABC123, tag your messages that don't come directly from you with "#TeamABC123."

As for the messages that *do* come directly from you, focus on keeping things "personal" and fun. This will help you build connection with fans, as they'll feel as if they know you.

Here are some suggestions for when you are doing your own social media:

1. Be Approachable

Being successful on Facebook, Twitter, or any other social media outlet is a lot like being successful in a bar: if you want people to talk to you, you need to be approachable. Showing your "human side" will help. An easy way for musicians to do this is to post candid photos and videos of "non-music" activities.

Examples:

- your tour bus at a drive-through window
- your van on the side of the road with a flat tire
- hanging out backstage
- your 5-star hotel room
- your 1-star hotel room

2. Give Value

Don't just bombard people with marketing messages of where you're playing, where your album is for sale, or requests to "vote" for you in some contest. Instead, let people know where they can get a free download of your music, where they can get photos of your current tour, or how they can be a part of your upcoming music video.

3. Start a Conversation

Social media isn't a one-way street, so don't just talk to people—talk with them. To do this, ask questions to better get to know your fans and focus on interaction, not revenue.

4. Think Beyond Text

Break up text-based tweets, messages, and blog posts with photos, audio, and video. A picture is worth a thousand words and, on average, will get more attention than a plain text message. In addition, bringing in audio and video to your social media keeps things fresh and will make *all* of your messages stand out more.

5. Ask for It!

Don't expect the person reading your message to also read your mind. If you want somebody to "like" it, respond to it, or share it with a friend, tell them what you want.

THE POWER OF SOCIAL MEDIA IN OFFLINE INTEGRATION

As exciting as social media and online interaction are, don't let anything you do online take away from the music you create and the offline activities you do, such as live performance. When integrated with offline activities, social media and online interaction become even more powerful.

Why? Because offline is where connections are made, friendships are strengthened, and true experience happens.

The UCLA Loneliness Scale, a tool based on a series of 20 questions designed to measure loneliness, has shown numbers rising dramatically over the last few years. According to a 2010 study by the AARP, 35 percent of adults over 45 were "chronically lonely." A UK study by the Mental Health Foundation suggested younger people were even more so.

As amazing as social media is, it can also be an isolating experience.

People want to be around other people. If you can help them to do that, using your music as a common theme, they will love you forever.

If you want a great example of this, look at Insane Clown Posse's fans, known as Juggalos. They have their own subculture, which goes way beyond Insane Clown Posse's music, and includes idioms, slang, and hairstyles. They have their own festival each year, The Gathering of the Juggalos, with 20,000 people attending.

Fans like these are why Insane Clown Posse is one of the top grossing independent acts, year after year.

If you've got a great online presence but don't have the kind of dedicated offline community that surrounds acts like Insane Clown Posse, a good first step in moving your online community in the offline direction is to add an online element to your live shows.

A simple yet effective example of how to make this happen is to have people in the audience of your shows take photos (of you or of each other) with their mobile phones and immediately upload them to Twitter using a hashtag dedicated to just that show. This will allow people who aren't attending to "participate" in real time, by leaving comments and sending messages to the people who are there.

This sets up interaction among your fans who are at the show, as well as among those who are online. It starts a connection between the two groups and will give social proof to those who aren't at the show that they're missing out, which will make them more likely to come next time.

A fan who is at a show, experiencing what you do in person, will almost always spend more money with you than a fan who is strictly online. Online interaction is easy, taking very little effort, while offline interaction requires a much greater amount of time, energy, and money. When people have to work to get something, they value it more.

The more hoops somebody is willing to go through to experience what you do, the more dedicated they are. Do what you can to encourage your online fans, such as friends on Facebook or followers on Twitter, to experience what you do offline. They'll have a more rewarding experience, and you'll make more money.

Ideally, you will do best with a blend of both online and offline fans. Keep them interested in what you're doing by moving them from an offline experience to something online and back again.

WELCOME TO THE VIP SECTION

Not all fans are equal. Some won't go beyond listening to you for free, whether that be via radio or another similar outlet. Many will buy only a single song. Others want all your albums. And a few will want everything you've ever recorded—from bootlegs to duets with other artists to alternative versions, such as dance mixes.

While you want to treat all your fans well, those who spend the most money should be treated especially well. You can do this by creating a fan club that offers members experiences, information, and merchandise that can't be found elsewhere.

The economics of a fan club can work a number of ways. Some are free. Others charge for a certain length of time. Both options can work, depending on your needs and where you are in your career.

If you are in the "building" phase of your music business career, where you have some fans but would like more, especially more *dedicated* fans, here is a fan club option that may work for you. This will help turn casual fans into more serious ones:

Price your fan club at $20 for a lifetime membership. In addition to fan club stuff, which I'll talk about below, give the buyer a package that includes your latest album, an exclusive album available only to fan club members, and an exclusive T-shirt. If you're selling memberships via live shows, throw in a free drink.

People love a bargain, and they love getting in on the ground floor of something. This offer gives them both.

With this offer, you're stacking what people receive so high, it's a no-brainer for them to sign up. Even if they're on the fence about you and your music, it's still a great deal, so something like this is a good way to turn casual fans into more dedicated ones.

A fan club doesn't just sell music and other merch; it sells a relationship between you and the member, as well as relationships among members. It's an instant family to which people can belong. Your fan club offer is a physical version of that to get fans started on the good feelings they get from these things.

Psychologically, people want two seemingly contradicting things:

1. **To Be Special** – We want to stand out and be different. We want something that says, "We're not like everybody else."

2. **To Be Accepted by a Group** – We want other people to like and value us.

A fan club provides both.

Fan clubs make people feel good, because they get special treatment. They also provide members with a feeling of superiority over "normal" fans.

You can do these things by providing the following:

- **Presale and Reserved Tickets** – If you're an act that tours in support of a specific album, I suggest giving away two tickets per tour to each fan club member. Have a special section just for fan club members, so they can associate with one another.

- **"Bring a Friend" Offers** – If you're playing a lot of local shows and constantly touring, I suggest "2-for-1" tickets. If you don't have a ticketing system and take money at the door, give members a "plus-one" card that lets them bring another person free with paid admission. This will not only fill your shows, but also encourage word of mouth.

- **"Meet and Greet Opportunities** – You should always meet with fans after a show, but if you have a fan club, arrange to have something specific for members that allows them more time with you or something everybody else can't get. For example, invite fans to a special acoustic performance or sound check before the show.

- **Members-Only Forums and Chat Rooms** – Fan club members will be more likely to remain active when they can interact with one another. An online forum or chat room also allows you to answer questions and keep in touch when you're not touring.

- **Exclusive Monthly Giveaways** – Give something away every month. This could be a guitar, stage clothing, or a personal item that isn't music related. It could be an experience, such as an opportunity to have dinner with you.

- **Exclusive Recordings** – A fan club is a great place to distribute work tapes, demos, and other recordings. If you're performing exclusive fan club shows, record and distribute them. Every year, release a holiday album.

- **Exclusive Merchandise** – Create an exclusive version of T-shirts or other merchandise for your fan club.

- **Exclusive Newsletter** – Postal mail is best, but email works. Regardless of how you send it, the content needs to be tailored specifically to the fan club and its more dedicated members. Q&A, tour diaries, photos with fan club members, a "member of the month" article, and new song lyrics are good places to start.

Remember, not all fans are equal. You'll make a lot more money off a small group of dedicated fans than a larger number of casual ones, so take great care of the people who are spending the most money with you, and go the extra mile to make sure they have a great experience.

You can learn a lot about fan clubs by joining the fan clubs of others.

Also watch companies that offer similar options to their customers, such as Zappos.com, Amazon, and American Express.

ONE WAY TO SCREW EVERYTHING UP AND LOSE ALL YOUR FANS

You must acknowledge your fans and those who support you on a regular basis. On social media outlets like Twitter and Facebook, everybody can see everything, so don't just focus on your "inner circle" of people in the business, close friends, and family. Bring your fans into the conversation.

You might be a bit freaked out by some fans, or, deep down, they may make you feel uncomfortable, because you feel undeserving of their attention. Get over it.

You must make your fans feel appreciated. They need to know you value them and their contributions to your music career. If you don't, they'll go away.

CONCLUSION

You fans want to connect with you. Reach out and give them that opportunity.

Your fans want to connect with one another. If you can facilitate this, with your music as the background noise, they will be forever loyal.

Integrate your online and offline marketing to be most effective. People are more lonely than ever and looking for ways to interact with one another online. At the same time, online social media is powerful and something that will make offline connections even stronger.

CHAPTER 6:

UNDERSTAND WHY PEOPLE BUY MUSIC

If you're not making money with music, it's because you're not connecting with fans in a strong enough way that makes them want to support you. Connection is the difference between a broke musician and a successful one.

Writing 12 good songs is a good start, but it's not enough.

"We Are the Champions" is a good song, but it was the *great* performance by Freddie Mercury that took it over the top. It was the energy he put into his studio recordings and live performances that made it connect with people. When he sang it, he meant it.

Freddie Mercury makes connecting with an audience seem effortless. A quick sampling of the dozens of available "We Are the Champion" covers will let you know it's more than a great song that made this happen, though.

Most of the time, it's not what you say but how you say it. The best song in the world, by itself, won't get you where you need to go. For that to happen, you have to give a little more.

Why people will support you:

- You give them a voice.

- You make them feel part of something.

- You provide a remedy for pain.

If you can do these things, you will make money in the music business.

THE MAJORITY OF PEOPLE ARE NOT LIKE YOU

You're a musician. You don't just listen to music; you *love* music. You also have a deep understanding of music, so when you listen to it, you're more open to experimenting with different styles and trying new artists than most people.

If you like an artist, it's likely that you have more than just his latest single or whatever is being played on the radio. In fact, if an artist you like has released more than one album, there is a good chance you have them.

If you know the music is out there, but it's not on the major sites like iTunes or Amazon, you'll go wherever you need to in order to get it. Not available as a download? You'll buy the CD. Not available on CD? You'll take the download. And if your options are really limited, you'll take a cassette or whatever else you can get your hands on.

In short, when it comes to getting the music you want, you'll jump through hoops and you're flexible.

As a musician, because you're so involved with music and love it so much, it's easy to think others feel the same way about it. This happens with people all the time: we think "they're just like us."

They're not.

Projecting our personal qualities on other people is part of our biology—it's a way for us to feel connected with people. It's such a firmly established habit for most of us, we do it without thinking.

One of my first jobs in the music business, other than playing in a band, was working at a record store. It was there that I learned the cold, hard reality of how most people feel about music.

Sure, there were some serious connoisseurs who took chances on the latest music from up-and-coming artists or dug deep into the catalogue to find rarities or lesser-known albums, but they were in the minority. The majority of people were more interested in already well-established, "middle of the road" artists like Kenny G, Celine Dion, and Michael Bolton. They wanted what was being played on the radio.

This is the depth of most people's music consumption. They want what they already know, and they're not interested in taking chances on anything else.

Assuming everybody will be just as excited about music as you are, when they're not, can be frustrating. Beyond that, making that assumption can cost you fans and money.

I learned this lesson while working as a DJ. I took a gig playing a private party and wrongly assumed the people there were like *my* people, club people.

They weren't.

I had a guy request something. I played a remixed version of it designed for the club.

Before the song was over, he came back to me and asked, "Can you play the one on the radio?"

It was the *same* song, yet a little different. Still, it was different enough to throw him off, and similar decisions that I made during that gig were enough for my booking agent to get complaints, which hurt my ability to get booked again.

I had forgotten a foundational rule of marketing—knowing who my audience was. It wasn't musicians and it wasn't club people; it was the general public—people who enjoyed music but wanted to hear what they were already familiar with.

HOW MOST PEOPLE THINK ABOUT MUSIC

The majority of music listeners fall into one of two categories:

- **Music Lovers** – These are the people who are *really* into music. They live and breathe it, it's a centerpiece of their social lives, and they'll do whatever it takes to get their hands on it. They're the type of people who shop at niche music stores, such as one for dance DJs, with specialty products that can't be found elsewhere, and they'll drive 300 (or more) miles to see a good show.

- **Casual Listeners** – Most people are here. They like music, but most of it is background noise for things they consider more important. If they purchase music, it's often just the single being played on the radio or a compilation album of singles, such as *Now That's What I Call Music!*

We've all met somebody who says he "likes" a certain artist, but if you follow that up with a question like, "Which song is your favorite?", the person can't name one.

Even worse, at least as far as selling music is concerned, are the people who have no clue about songs or who is singing them. Music consumption ends when they turn off the radio. And these people are more common than you'd think. When asked about the type of music they listen to, they answer, "Whatever is on the radio."

The music lover will gladly pay to stream unlimited, commercial-free music to a mobile device. The casual listener, if streaming music at all, is happy to sit through commercials and have limited music access in order to save the money.

Most people purchase music the way most people purchase books.

True book lovers are the kind of people who walk into a bookstore and look through the shelves, browsing their favorite genre, picking through stacks of books, looking for something new and exciting to read. Mystery lovers will take a chance on something based on a cover, title, or "Employee Pick" selection. Those who love classic literature may purchase something that has been reissued with new commentary or perhaps a hardcover of a paperback they've already read.

The average book buyer may be a fan of a movie star, sports figure, or politician, which will get him to buy. For example, if he likes wrestling and sees a book by Hulk Hogan, he'll at least check it out. Or if she really loved Guns N' Roses, a book by Slash would get his attention.

The average book buyer gets books at stores like Target or Wal-Mart. He's there buying things like an iron, some shampoo, or batteries. Any books being purchased are an afterthought that wouldn't have crossed his mind at all had the book not gotten to the place where the book seems "everywhere" and everybody is talking about it.

Harry Potter was like that.

Twilight was like that.

Sarah Palin's book *Rogue* was like that.

The majority of the "big albums" are similar. General consumers, not true fans, pushed things over the top.

Although this can and does happen, it rarely happens. Your odds of "music business success" will be far greater if you stop worrying about making everybody happy and focus on finding and developing true fans instead of casual music buyers. True fans are the people who start the ball rolling, spend more money on music than the general population, and will stick with you for a long time.

KNOW WHAT YOU'RE SELLING

What people buy and what they say they buy are, almost always, two different things. For example, nobody just buys a new car. When somebody gets a new car, he is buying:

- Status

- Ease

- Sex Appeal

- An Ego Boost

A new car is actually a "middleman" standing in the way. If there is an easier way to get these things, or if the person already has them, there is no need for the car.

By this same token, nobody simply buys music. Most of the time, they are purchasing the feeling they get while listening to that music. For example, the relaxation they feel when listening to some gentle New Age music or the rebelliousness they feel when listening to a gangsta rapper's opinion of the police.

Music is a soundtrack to our lives. It's what's playing in the background when we're doing other things, because it helps to facilitate these other things.

Archie Bell said it best ...

Just think, no more dancing
no, no, no people dancing to the beat
They'd be no birdy to wake you in the morning
with a sweet, sweet melody

Music is what adds value to everything else we do in life. You could still dance *without* music, but it wouldn't be nearly as fun. And although birds can be very beautiful just to look at, the songs they sing add an entirely different element to that beauty, since they involve another sense.

That is the power of music. It adds a sonic element to everything else we have going on, which makes everyday experiences even more powerful. When you know this is what you're selling, your marketing efforts will become even more powerful as well.

HOW TO GO BIG

Consumers, for the most part, are "checked out" when it comes to music. They simply want to be entertained, and they have thousands of entertainment options, most of which *aren't* music.

Should they go see a band? Should they watch a movie instead? Why do that when you can pull out your phone and play a game of Angry Birds?

People are overwhelmed with entertainment choices.

How can you be the one they pick?

You want to be so entertaining that, even if somebody doesn't like your music, your talent won't be questioned. When you're this good, not only will you cut through the noise of tens of thousands of other acts releasing music each week, but you'll cut through the noise going on in the average consumer's head, forcing him to sit up and take notice of you.

The type of acts at this level are the ones we consider classic. They're so revered that, even after they've broken up, retired, or even dead, they still make money.

Examples of acts like this include:

- Michael Jackson

- Queen

- Elvis

- The Beatles

- Jimi Hendrix

- Led Zeppelin

- ABBA

People like these acts for different reasons, such as quality showmanship, depth of lyrics, raw energy of performances, and camaraderie that happens between the artist and audience during live shows. Underneath that, though, and most important, is the *feeling of connection* people experience when they think about the act. They feel understood.

Most people never get to that level. For those who do, it often takes years.

Depressing, isn't it?

Here's the good news ...

This is not an "all-or-nothing" business. If you can connect with an audience, you can still make good money with your music and have a very successful career, even if you aren't internationally famous. And, even better, you don't have to wait years to start doing it.

The trick is to start with where you are, building your fan base one person at a time.

How do you accomplish this?

Love your fans.

Songs are a starting point. A "good song" will sell records, but it won't get you a career.

The secret to a long career is treating your fans well and making them feel good.

People don't buy music, go to shows, or otherwise support your music business because you're involved; they spend their money, their time, and their energy on you because of the way you make them feel.

And how you make them feel is *everything* ...

THE POWER OF MAKING PEOPLE FEEL GOOD

I once met a guy who had just moved to town. He was 30-something and without a job and didn't even have his own place: he was renting a room in somebody else's house.

Within a couple of weeks, one of my friends was totally in love with him. Soon after, another one of my friends was in the mix. And there were several other women just like them, not just in Nashville, but all over the country.

The guy was a jerk, had no money, and wasn't very good looking. How could something like this happen?

He was a good listener.

The women involved with him knew none of the things I knew, because when he was with them, he'd shut up and let them do the talking. Because so few men do this, it was easy for them to be won over. In addition, they filled in the "blank space" he gave them with all the great things they imagined him to be.

The women who dated this guy weren't idiots. Had you asked any of them if they'd date a guy who was over 30 and living in the equivalent of his mother's basement, the answer you would have received would have been something like, "Hell no."

Yet here they were ... fighting over one another to be with that kind of guy.

That is the power of making somebody feel good. And that's the power you have when interacting with your fans.

You don't have to be a great musician to be successful in the music business; you just have to be good with people.

A great example of this is KISS. Not the best songs in the world and certainly not the deepest lyrics, but they put on a great show in which fans are thanked multiple times throughout.

The result is that KISS has had 30+ years of Gold and Platinum albums. Even when they're not on the radio, they still sell records and sell out auditoriums. Beyond the music, there are the over 2,000 products they've licensed their name and image to, including condoms, lunch boxes, Halloween costumes, vacation packages, pinball machines, video games, and credit cards.

Jimmy Buffett has a similar philosophy. When you go to a Jimmy Buffett show, you don't see him on the JumboTron, you see the audience. He builds community by making his fans part of the show. Then he sells them everything from T-shirts to food to home décor ... and they love it!

Going to the extremes of KISS or Jimmy Buffett isn't for everybody, but with the changing climate of the music business, where music is just as easily pirated as purchased legally, merchandising is keeping a lot of musicians in business. Beyond that, it's keeping a lot of fans happy.

As a musician, part of your job is to give somebody a voice. Whether it's a housewife in the middle of Kansas or an awkward kid who gets picked on at his school, you're saying what somebody wants to say, but feels like he can't.

Merchandise isn't you putting your name or logo on everything you possibly can in order to make more money, although money is certainly one of the secondary payoffs. For most people, it's something that allows them to take home a piece of what they've experienced at a live show or expand on what they feel when they hear a song. And whether or not people realize it, it's also something that allows them to communicate a message they wouldn't otherwise be able to.

Help them out!

WHAT PEOPLE WANT

If you've ever been to a wedding reception with a DJ playing music, you've likely heard a few of these songs on the playlist ...

- "YMCA" by The Village People

- "Cupid Shuffle" by Cupid

- "Electric Boogie" (also known as "The Electric Slide") by Marcia Griffiths

- "Cha Cha Slide" by Mr. C

- "The Twist" by Chubby Checker

Why? Let's break it down ...

First of all, each of these songs was (and still is) popular. Part of the reason for that is because each has a dance associated with it that is simple, easy to learn, and "inclusive." Even if you're not a "dancer" and sit still during every other song being played, you can participate when these come on without feeling like a fool.

People want to be part of the show. They want to connect with other people. Dancing together lets them do that.

These songs get played a lot because they make people feel good. If you can do the same through your songs, they'll be played too.

Remember these two words: Be inclusive.

Songs that bring people together aren't limited to those that have dances associated with them. Want something even better that will last long after you do? Write an anthem.

An anthem speaks to a specific group of people, based on gender, economic background, political beliefs, sexual orientation, or any other demographic information and says exactly what they're feeling in a way they can't.

An anthem is more than a song. It's more than a hit single.

Anthems aren't limited to a specific style or genre; they come in all forms. The main characteristic that links them together is some form of synchronized audience participation (often a sing-along chorus or other hook).

Examples of arena songs:

- "Another One Bites the Dust" by Queen
- "T.N.T." by AC/DC
- "Rock and Roll (Part 2)" by Gary Glitter
- "Na Na Hey Hey Kiss Him Goodbye" by Steam
- "All Star" by Smash Mouth

An anthem gives people a voice. It's a rallying cry that gets everybody in the club, the stadium, or wherever else up on their feet and involved in the performance.

Here are common themes found in this type of song:

- **Overcoming Hardship** – These are often money related.
  - You were broke once, but now you're rich.
  - You used to live in the ghetto (or were homeless) and now you live in a mansion.

- **Overcoming Oppression** – Can be everything from political to parents to sexual orientation.

  - Your country was occupied but is now free.

  - You were in a controlling relationship, but you got away.

- **You Are Not Alone** – Young? Pregnant? Gay? You're not the only one.

- **Forgot Your Problems** – Job sucks? Lover left you? Broke? None of it matters now.

- **Rebellion and Defiance** – Can be political or social in nature.

  - Your father says you're too young to date, but you're not going to let that stop you.

  - Marijuana is illegal, but you're going to smoke it anyway.

- **Survival** – You will never give in.

  - You get knocked down, but you get up again.

  - 25 miles to go? Feet hurtin' mighty bad? Got to keep on walkin'.

- **Not Giving Up** – These often have to do with love or struggle.

  - When you get out of jail in 50 years, I promise I'll be here.

  - It hurts like hell, but I'm going to keep on pushing.

- **Freedom** – Often political but not always. Lots of "biker songs" fall into the category.

If you want to see anthems in action, go to one of two places: a karaoke night at your local bar or a drag show.

When a pissed-off woman gets onstage during karaoke night and sings "Respect" by Aretha Franklin, it's more than just a performance. She's saying everything she hasn't been able to say until then, and the friends she's brought with her are there to back her up.

When a drag queen performs to "I Will Survive" by Gloria Gaynor, watch the audience. Look at their reaction and the determination on their faces. They're feeling *every* word.

How can you get this kind of reaction from *your* audience?

Finally, similar in terms of how lyrics connect with an audience, is a type of song I call "remedy for pain." These songs are usually based on a specific situation a listener is dealing with or larger-scale events that affect many people (such as natural disasters, political situations or war).

The best examples of these songs come from artists who are completely tapped into their audiences and know how those people are feeling.

Examples of "remedy for pain" songs:

- John Cougar Mellencamp's "Rain on the Scarecrow," written about the farming crisis that hit the Midwest United States in the 1980s.

- Toby Keith's "Courtesy of the Red, White, and Blue" was released after the September 11 attacks in 2001.

- For decades, Johnny Paycheck's "Take This Job and Shove It" has been a rally cry for those who are fed up with their jobs.

What pain does *your* audience need a remedy for?

To summarize, songs with one or more of the following elements will have the best shot at doing well because they will truly resonate with your audience:

- **A Dance People Can Do** – Moving to music is one of our most primal urges, yet dancing in public, for many people, is a huge fear.

Create a simple dance that goes along with your song. It should have rules. People want to participate, but they're scared to death of looking like idiots, so let them know what to do. Bonus points if you can give the rules within the song, like "Cupid Shuffle" by Cupid or "Cha Cha Slide" by Mr. C.

- **A Hook People Can Sing** – Like dancing, singing along makes a song interactive. The problem is that most have limited, if any, singing ability. The more you can work with this, the better chance of success your song has.

  Examples of this include "Sweet Caroline" by Neil Diamond and "American Pie" by Don McLean.

- **Lyrics People Can Relate To** – If you can write a "generic" song that a lot of people feel is about them, you've got a hit. "Amazed" by Lonestar and "Let's Stay Together" by Al Green are great examples of this. For more, look at common "first dance" songs played during weddings.

If you can connect with people like this, you will make a good living in the music business.

THIS IS NEVER ABOUT YOU

Fans make the decision about whether you're "good" or not. They don't care about artistic elements of what you do, the quality of your songwriting, or the complexities of putting on a show. The only thing that matters is how you, your actions, and your music make them feel.

Fans don't care about the "business" of the music industry. They don't care that, when you're off stage, you have a thousand little things that need to be working properly in order for you to get to the next show, record your next album, write your best songs, or live a comfortable life.

Fans want to feel energized and inspired, they want a voice, they want to be included, and they want a remedy for pain. You have the opportunity to provide all of these things with a "fantasy" that takes them away from the jobs they hate, dealing with bad relationships, and trying to make ends meet.

If you can do this, not just with your music but also in your marketing, it will change your career.

How can you give them a voice? Ask them for opinions on the "fun" aspects of your career, such as the design of your next album cover, or letting them pick the songs you'll perform during a gig.

How can you include them in what you're doing? A good way to start is by acknowledging specific fans in blog posts, posting fan photos in social media, and replying to fan questions via Twitter.

How can you provide a remedy for their pain? Give them live events where they have a fun time, connecting with old friends and meeting new ones.

There is one question you should ask yourself before you do anything (and I mean do *anything*) involving your music business career—from the songs you write, to the art you use for your new album, to the interviews that you do, even the way you perform, and, especially, the way you interact with people:

"Will this make my fans feel good?"

Do you like buying music on vinyl because you enjoy looking at the liner notes? Great. Don't assume your fans feel the same way, though. Ask first.

It doesn't matter that you hate Apple. If your fans prefer to buy music via iTunes, let them.

Do your fans like to record your shows and trade them with other fans? Find a way to make it work.

If it makes your fans feel good, don't fight it. It's much easier to go with the momentum.

The bottom line is that there is knowledge to be gained from listening to your fans that you can use to your advantage. Forget the market research, focus groups of just a few people, or "professional" opinions. Your fans know what they want, and if you give it to them, you'll always do well.

Keeping connected to fans like this will not only help with the ease in which you grow your music business, but it will also help you to keep your street credibility.

Fans want to know that you care for them. That's a lot easier when you're running your own career, but when you bring in managers and other "professionals" who start taking over different aspects of your business, it's easy to become disconnected from that.

The problem many bands face when taking things up a notch is that they stop doing the things that got them where they are. No more selling their own merchandise, signing autographs, taking requests, responding to emails, crashing with fans, hanging out at the bar after a show, or any of the little things that made people feel a connection. Instead, they try to do everything on a much bigger, "us to them" level that treats people as a nameless, faceless group rather than a collective of individuals.

As your career grows, of course you're going to have to change the way you approach things. Personally responding to emails isn't a good option for long. Selling your own merchandise works better in a small club than a theater or arena. Staying in a hotel is easier and quicker than crashing with fans.

But don't let scaling your business keep your fans out of the conversation.

Forget trying to please record labels, publishing companies, or the music media. Fans have the ultimate decision over whether you succeed or fail. When you please your fans, everybody else will come around.

Fans drive everything. When the fans are happy, everybody is happy.

So anything you do from this point on should be prefaced with the question, "Will this make my fans feel good?"

On a related note, this strategy works with more than just fans. It works with labels, music supervisors, music publishers, booking agents, club owners, sponsorship people, *American Idol* judges, and everybody you'll ever run into.

Find out what your audience wants and give it to them.

If you make your fans feel good enough, they may just turn into superfans. One of the reasons this happens is that you're making fans feel like they're part of the process. Instead of ignoring them, which is what most acts do, you're building loyalty by bringing them into the conversation.

The relationship you have with fans is not unlike that of an employer and employee. If an employer listens to employee complaints, suggestions and comments, the employees are much more loyal than if he completely ignores them.

It sounds counterintuitive, but allowing fans to actually do work for you, whether it be designing album art, helping to promote an upcoming show, or picking the name of your new record, even if the work they do is free of charge, will actually make fans more excited about what you're doing. You get to benefit from the wisdom of crowds as well as increased loyalty from your audience.

YOUR RELATIONSHIP WITH FANS

The reality is, when it comes to your day-to-day life, you have more in common with your fans than they realize. You've got relationship issues, bills, and the same issues as they do. In addition, you're dealing with aspects of the music business that aren't as fun as they appear to outsiders.

This doesn't matter.

Fans want to be entertained. Period. Don't burden them with more problems.

Fans want to know you, and they want to be part of your success. It's fine to share parts of your life with them, but if you share a personal problem of yours, make sure it's handled and the story ends on a positive note.

For example, if you have a flat tire on the way to a show, don't get on stage, on Twitter, or anywhere else and complain about it. Don't let people know you'll be sleeping in the van for the next week because you spent all your money on a tow and a tire.

Instead, make something like this an *adventure*. It's a situation that, when fixed, shows your fans how much you'll go through to put on a good show for them.

POST THIS: "Had a flat tire today. Paid off the mechanic to fix it fast!! No way were we going to miss playing for CLEVELAND tonight!"

DON'T POST THIS: "Had a flat tire today. Messed up the rim. Cost us a ton. Gig was lame. OHIO SUCKS!!!"

If you can make people feel good, feel included and give them an escape from things they don't like, you can make a good living in the music business. In the end, that's all that matters to them.

THE "SUPERFAN"

We've all known "superfans" who feel a huge connection to their favorite bands. If you can cultivate this type of relationship with your fans, you'll have massive loyalty that will last for as long as you want to put out music.

So how do you create superfans?

If your goal is to cultivate a group of superfans, you'll have an easier time going "narrow and deep" with your music and activities than "shallow and wide."

Barry White did this. I once heard an interview with him in which he said, "I've written hundreds of songs … and every single one of them is about love."

That is "narrow and deep."

If you like love songs done in a soul and disco style, Barry White is your man.

Would it make sense for Barry White to do show tunes? Hair metal? Reggae?

No.

Yet this is the equivalent of what many musicians do when they jump around, changing musical styles or lyrical content. One minute they're heavy, the next minute they're going for something pop, so they can get radio play.

Over the years, I've met several upcoming musicians who are playing in more than one band, recording songs in various styles, or otherwise trying to put a lot of different chips on the table. And like a lot of chips on the table, you may have something come up a winner, but it's doubtful it will get you the result you're looking for.

If that "radio hit" takes off, do you think people would be converted to the heavy stuff? No. Instead, people would buy the album and be pissed the rest of it isn't like what they heard on the radio.

Being all over the place confuses people. People love Barry White because they know what they get when they purchase a Barry White record. They don't get songs about politics, the environment, or social issues; they get songs about love. And the style isn't country or rock or salsa; the style is always based in R&B or soul.

Barry White sings about the things that his fans are feeling—or want to feel. And he's skilled at it, delivering the message in a way that most people would never be able to.

I'm not talking about his baritone voice; I'm talking about his on-point message and delivery. It's *exactly* what needs to be said, delivered in a perfect way.

Other acts that have done this well:

- Erasure
- Cypress Hill
- Morrissey
- DC Talk
- Iron Maiden
- Henry Rollins
- Sammy Hagar
- Jimmy Buffett
- The Black Crowes
- Toby Keith

The deeper you go with your message, the deeper relationship you'll have with fans.

HONESTY WILL TAKE YOU A LONG WAY

In 2006, Meghan Tonjes started posting original music videos on YouTube. Soon after, she was taking requests for cover versions of popular (and not so popular) songs.

Word of her talent spread and, with the help of top social media personalities such as Perez Hilton, Ryan Seacrest, and Ellen DeGeneres, her videos have been seen over 10 million times, with over 150,000 people subscribing to her YouTube channel.

At the beginning of 2011, she performed on *The Ellen DeGeneres Show*. Within a few days, her debut album, *Be In Want*, hit number eight on the iTunes Singer-Songwriter chart. It was one of the top 20 most downloaded albums that week (right below Tracy Chapman and Sheryl Crow).

Plenty of musicians have put videos on YouTube. Plenty of YouTube videos have been featured by Perez Hilton. Ellen DeGeneres often showcases YouTube successes on her show.

Most never see the success that Meghan Tonjes has.

So what is it that makes her different?

Part of it may be her appearance and how she relates to people. She's not slick in the way most people think of successful musicians. She's an "every girl" who just so happens to have an amazing voice.

She's also honest.

When she appeared on *The Ellen DeGeneres Show*, she didn't just perform songs. She talked about being bullied when growing up due to her size and how it was still happening online.

When she makes non-music videos for YouTube, she gets personal, talking about weight loss, family issues, and more. She shares everything from the books she is reading to her skincare routine to her experience with back problems.

In one video, she's naked on a hotel room bed.

She's inspiring, even though she has flaws. And those flaws don't repel people; they attract people.

People wish they had the guts to be known in the way she's allowed herself to be known.

They wish they had the guts to be as honest with the world as she is.

They wish they could be as fearless.

There is a big difference between this and the "honesty" that many musicians share. Megan Tonjes expresses herself while adding to the fantasy people have about musicians and the music business.

Megan Tonjes is the "small-town girl done good" who inspires her listeners and lets them know what is possible. Like her, like all of us, they're flawed. If she can do it, we all can.

Remember, you are the voice of your audience. Sometimes that's through lyrics they can relate to, but sometimes it's simply by being successful as yourself.

Letting people know what's possible is perhaps the most powerful message of all.

CONCLUSION

You're a musician. Most people don't like music in the way that you do. Because of this, you need to approach creating and marketing your music in a way that appeals to them.

We all have dreams, hopes, and insecurities. If you can tap into these things and express them better than the people listening to your music can express themselves, you will connect with them in a way so powerful that they'll follow you to the end of the world and back.

This is the reason people buy music.

CHAPTER 7:

RISE ABOVE
THE NOISE

The Internet is a great tool for musicians, but it's far from the level playing field so many have claimed. Fortunately for you, this is something that can work to your advantage.

If everybody in the room is shouting, nobody can hear what you're saying.

This is how the Internet is for most musicians. It's like they're standing in a stadium full of other musicians, with everybody holding up copies of their albums, hoping somebody will pay attention to them.

The problem is twofold. One, because everybody is shouting themselves, nobody can hear you. Two, you're surrounded by people who are in the same position you are, and these people don't buy music because they're too busy making their own.

Where are the music buyers?

The music buyers are in a totally different stadium—the one with the bands who have successfully broken through the noise. Those bands are playing a different game than indie bands, and most of them got there with the help of major press, major radio, major television appearances, and things the average independent artist has little hope of making happen.

The "filters" that musicians used to have to work around—television, radio, and other traditional media—were actually a good thing in many ways. The system didn't have room for everybody, but for those who were able to get inside, the odds of success were much better than they are today, because there were fewer bands to compete with.

It's not that you can't compete with the noise. You can. You're not going to do it by shouting louder than the rest of the people, though—that's impossible. The only way to cut through the noise is to be smarter with your marketing, be more knowledgeable about your audience (and what they want), and have a product that people will connect with in such an intense way, the next logical decision is for them to purchase it.

How do you begin taking your marketing to the point where you can compete with the noise?

It starts with *you* …

HOW TO COMPETE (AND WIN) IN THE MUSIC BUSINESS

There are three things (and one is optional) that will make you stand out among the hundreds of thousands of aspiring musicians who also want to "make it." This is so simple, you may look at it and think, "I'm already doing these things," but keep in mind that, even if you're doing them on a major level, there is *always* a step beyond where you are now, and I encourage you to keep looking to push your limits and increase your ability to do these things.

Be Interesting

This is going to be harsh, but it's important. It's the biggest misconception that many musicians have about what they're doing and the top reason the majority of acts fail.

Keep this in mind at all times:

Choosing to become involved with a project doesn't automatically make it interesting to other people.

The funny (and perhaps ironic) twist to this is that, while many people may not find your choice in projects interesting, there are elements about you and your life that many people would find fascinating. You may find your day-to-day rituals boring or take your most endearing personality traits for granted, but other people won't.

For example, if you've got a fake leg, that's not ground-breaking, but it *is* interesting, because it helps tell a story that will allow fans to go deeper in their connection to you.

If you started performing music when you were 15 and had to sneak into the venue to play your own gigs, that's interesting. Any details about you and your life that will help people better understand you and give them insight into the music they love will make them have greater appreciation for what you do.

Are you approaching your music career in a unique way? That can be interesting to people.

Maybe there is something about the way you make music that is different from how most people make music. For example, if you recorded your new album in your car, that's interesting. Did you use your iPhone to do it? Even better, because there are millions of iPhone fanatics who are a built-in audience for something like this.

The point is, if you want a lot of attention for your music, you need to think about more than just the music itself. By definition, all musicians make music. You need to offer more—a personality and story people will connect with. This is what will differentiate your music from what everybody else is doing.

Examples:

- Jewel grew up in Alaska, she yodels, and she used to live in her van.

- Eminem has an ex-wife named Kim and a daughter named Hailie.

- Bo Diddley played a square guitar.

- Sting does yoga, and, because of this, can have sex for 14 hours without stopping.

- Ted Nugent kills endangered animals with a crossbow.

These examples, like the ones you'll use to connect people to your music in a deeper way, are pretty basic and hardly flashy. They're easy to overlook.

What you find interesting about yourself and what other people find interesting about you are often two different things. Because of this, you may find it helpful to ask friends, family members, and others whom you're close with for their opinions. You may be sitting on great stories that you don't know are great because you're too close to them.

If you can find something that appears to be a contradiction, that is great. I once met a romance writer who used to be a nun. That got a lot of people curious about what she was writing.

Once you have something unique that you feel people will find of interest, simply share it during interviews, posts on social media, or interaction with fans. It doesn't need to become your identity; just mention it casually or even downplay it for best results.

Be Entertaining

You need to be entertaining. This means that you need to do something beyond simply playing music.

If you want to see what "just playing music" is like, go to YouTube and look up "Lawrence Welk Show." The performers on this program were great musicians, and what they did worked well at the time, but people today want more than "just playing music."

Ask somebody on his way to a music performance to describe what he's about to do and he'll say, "I'm going to *see* a show."

If you want to be successful in the music business, you need to give it to him.

This doesn't mean you need a dozen costume changes or six dancers behind you or fireworks; it simply means that, if you want to hold people's attention, you'll need to deliver something beyond just sitting there and playing music when you're on stage.

How can you give people more than just a music performance? One way is to make people part of the show.

The Internet, video games, and technology such as iPhones have changed the way we think about entertainment. It's no longer interesting for us to just watch something; we want to interact with it.

The reason dance music is so popular is that it allows the audience to be part of the show.

The most popular songs ever are the ones we can sing along with.

The churches with the highest attendance are the ones where the congregation interacts with the minister, the choir, and the other "performers."

Use this same concept in your music. Even though your name is on everything, move away from the one-way broadcast most musicians use (in which the focus would solely be on you) into a two-way "relationship" between you and your fans, where they also add to, and play a role in, the experience.

Be a Good Musician (OPTIONAL)

If you want to be known as a good musician, being able to play well is important. If you want to make money as a musician, playing well is further down the list.

In general, people don't go see shows because there is a good musician on stage. They go see shows because of how the experience makes them feel. Being a good musician may actually stand in the way of this.

As an example, if you play classical guitar the traditional way, which most classical guitarists do, you're seated in a chair, your back is straight, and you have one foot on a small footstool in order to angle the guitar a certain way. This position allows you to play more easily than other positions, such as standing with the guitar strapped over your shoulder.

But a guitar strapped over your shoulder allows you to connect with people. You can run around the stage, you can take your hands off the guitar, and you can jump up and down, encouraging the audience to do the same.

Some of the most memorable moments during a live show come from when an audience member gets pulled up on stage. Would this ever happen during a classical performance? Absolutely not. Why? It can screw up the musicality of the show.

Nobody talks about "musicality" or "musicianship" when they're describing how they were feeling when they saw an enthusiastic fan get plucked from the audience to help sing backup vocals. Those situations have nothing to do with music; they're about letting people be part of something.

If you're playing any style of contemporary music (i.e., almost everything but classical), keep this in mind. You are not a musician as much as you are a catalyst for people to feel something.

Am I saying you should ditch playing your instrument and rely solely on pitch correction or other technology to fill in your weak spots? Absolutely not. Being able to play well can only help you in your music business career. Don't think it's all that you need, though, and don't make it a more important aspect of your music business than it actually is.

Remember, what you're really selling is a feeling. Music is only the middleman.

DIGITAL MUSIC IS INVISIBLE

Digital music has a lot of things going for it. You can get it instantly, from anywhere in the world, provided you have an online connection. There are no manufacturing costs, a service like iTunes can handle 10,000 sales as easily as it can handle one, and sound quality doesn't deteriorate after multiple plays.

However, there is a major downside for musicians and record labels.

Simply put, "iPods don't advertise."

Nobody knows what the guy with an iPod, or mobile phone, or other portable music device is listening to. That's much different than in years past, when people would carry around a briefcase full of cassettes or a CD binder. There is no longer a physical product to hold, flip through, or pass around.

Because of this, musicians and record labels are missing out on valuable promotion.

Here are five ways you can get people talking about you and your music:

- **The 2-for-1** – Just to be clear, this is where you offer two of the *same item* for the same price it would cost to purchase one. This is done with the intention that the buyer will pass along the extra copy to a friend, thus spreading the word about you and your music.

When you make an offer like this, be clear that you want people to tell their friends about you and pass your music along. Don't expect them to read your mind.

Here are a couple of example scripts you can recite from stage to help encourage this action:

> *"This is our first time in <<CITY>>, and we need your help getting the word out about what's happened here. Tonight only, when you buy our new album for $10, we're going to give you a second copy free. This is so you can take it to your work or school tomorrow and give it to a friend who appreciates good music."*

> *"This is for the men in the audience tonight ... I got a trick that will make you 10x hotter to women. Tonight only, when you buy my new album for $10, I'm going to give you a second copy free. This is so, tomorrow, when you go to work or school, you'll be able to go up to the hottest woman in the place and give her a copy. Trust me, it works. OK, seriously, this is my first time in <<CITY>> and I could use your help getting the word out about what's happened here. $10 and you'll get a little something for yourself, plus impress a friend with your generosity."*

Although this promotion was designed to encourage word of mouth, one of the reasons this promotion will help you sell more music is that most people don't go to see music alone and it's likely that you'll have people in the audience who "split" the deal. That's fine. You're attaching yourself to an existing friendship, and your offer is helping to create a shared experience with your music as the centerpiece.

- **T-Shirts** – Every musician needs to have T-shirts available for sale. They help get the word out about what you're doing, start conversations about you and your music, and connect fans to one another. In addition, they're great items to include in "combo" deals, as well as in press kits to help you stand out.

- **Photos** – With the rise of online social media, photos are the perfect way to get the word out about your band. Don't just "allow" photos to be taken—encourage the activity. Then go one more step and encourage people to share their photos with others.

  For example:

  "We want to see all the photos you take tonight. When you upload them to Facebook, make sure you tag each one with <<BAND NAME>>, so we can add them to our photo gallery."

- **Live Tapes** – People attending a live show want to take home something that will allow them to relive the experience and share it with others. A live recording of the show is a great way to do both.

  Allowing people the opportunity to get a high-quality, official recording of your show in exchange for an email address or other contact information is a good way to build a mailing list. In addition, having a collection of live recordings will also give you multiple options for releasing paid content.

- **Live Videos** – YouTube is the number-one music search engine. Lana Del Rey performed on *Saturday Night Live* based on her success on YouTube. Search "record deal from YouTube" on Google and you'll see multiple acts that have done just that. The a cappella group Straight, No Chaser not only got a record deal but has toured nationally—all because of a 10 year-old video one of the members found and decided to put online.

  If you're not on YouTube, you're missing out on a great opportunity to attract potential fans as well as keep current fans engaged. And allowing the people who come see your live show to record video and upload it is the ultimate form of leverage.

THE DRIP METHOD

When the primary way of distributing music was physical, such as CDs, vinyl records, and cassettes, it made economic sense to release an entire album full of music. This was because CDs, vinyl records, and cassettes with a single song cost the same amount to manufacture and distribute as CDs, vinyl records, and cassettes with 10 or more songs but could be sold for only a fraction of the price.

Today, because the majority of music is being distributed through online outlets, we no longer have these problems. We can produce as many copies as the public demands without worrying about "manufacturing" costs, finding a truck big enough to ship everything in, or limited shelf space.

The downside of that is that releasing music has gotten so easy that there is a lot of noise to cut through. More and more music is being released each week, and the number is only going to continue to grow as it gets easier and easier to record new music and older, catalogued music is added to digital music outlets.

For most acts, it's no longer a good idea to keep fans waiting a year or more between new albums. Because they're being flooded with music and non-music entertainment options, the half-life of music (and the artists who make it) is becoming shorter and shorter.

You can stay competitive and appease the short attention spans of your audience by putting out music on a more frequent basis. Release songs soon after they are recorded. Don't wait until you have enough songs to fill an entire album. This is something I refer to as "The Drip Method," because, rather than giving people all your songs in a single collection with one big push, you release them individually, over a longer period of time.

In other words, you are *constantly* releasing new music in order to keep fans engaged and make sure they don't forget about you. You can then take your best songs from the process, which will have already been tested, to create strong, full-length albums, to market to new fans as they come along as well as your hardcore fans, who want everything you put out, even if they already have a similar version.

Here are five reasons I recommend releasing single songs as they are written and recorded ...

A new release is a good reason to reach out to (and connect with) fans.

At its core, the drip method makes sense because it gives you a good reason to communicate and build rapport with fans. Not only do you have a good excuse to contact people to let them know that your latest song is available for sale, but you also have several great opportunities to connect with and relate to fans when you are in the creation process.

Assuming you make the drip method part of your ongoing marketing strategy, meaning that you choose to *constantly* be in the process of releasing new music, here are a few things that will help you build tremendous rapport with your fans:

- Ask fans who attend your live shows and have heard new material, which song you should record next.

- Ask for opinions on the artwork you use. Or better yet, allow fans to submit their designs for you to use.

- Allow fans to sing background vocals, provide hand claps, or otherwise be part of the recording process.

- Allow fans to watch you record, either in-person or via webcam.

It allows you to test songs.

It's always a big deal to fans when you put out new music, but a single song isn't as big of a deal as an entire album, so if you're going to screw up a song, it's much better to do it as part of an ongoing stream of single recordings via the drip method, where you can quickly get it off the market, than as part of a multi-song album, where it will take away from the other, much better songs in the collection.

The drip method will allow you a little more flexibility in the recordings you release and give you more breathing space should something tank.

Being on the road and performing new music for different crowds who attend your live shows is a solid way of testing new material, but if you want to know how well a *recording* of a song will be received, the best way to find out is by releasing it to all your fans. Not only can you get feedback, but it allows your fans to feel like they're part of your creative process. It also gives your superfans a reason to get the word out about what you're doing.

It keeps you moving forward.

Have you ever seen people who go from one extreme to another? For example, if they need to lose a few pounds, they'll go on a really strict diet or lock themselves in the gym for a while. Then, when the pounds come off, it's back to business as usual.

One week it's fried cheese and Twinkies. The next week it's raw veggies and cardio machines. Then it's back to fried cheese and Twinkies ... until the cycle starts again.

The result is that, in the end, absolutely nothing gets accomplished. It's a lot of *action*, but not forward momentum, because they always seem to end up right where they started.

This is how most musicians operate. They'll do nothing for a few months, or even years, then do a ton of gigs or record a ton of songs in a short amount of time, only to go back to doing nothing shortly thereafter.

Not only does this not work from a business standpoint, it doesn't work from a creative one. When you "start over" with a new album or tour, you waste a lot of energy getting back momentum you once had. Being consistent, on the other hand, allows you to keep promotion momentum going as well as keep your creative "muscle" in shape, which means you'll be much more efficient writing and recording great songs.

The most successful musicians I've ever seen follow the rule of ABC: Always Be Creating.

It helps with cash flow.

Releasing music via the drip method also makes good financial sense. Constantly releasing single songs (as opposed to releasing an entire album of material less frequently) allows for more consistent income, not only from music sales, but also live dates, as you'll be able to record your album in short spurts, without taking a lot (if any) time off the road.

You'll make more money.

Thanks to iTunes, the Android Marketplace, and Apple's App Store, people are very comfortable buying something for $0.99. They're also comfortable taking chances on new products, like music, because the price is so low.

"Less risk" means a greater chance that somebody will buy your music. The really exciting part about selling music on a per-song basis, though, is that, in the end, you'll make more money than if you were to sell the entire album as single product.

Let's do the math ...

Entire albums sell for as little as $5. If you have 10 songs and sell them individually for $0.99 each, that's $9.90, almost twice as much. It's the same method that allows "by the slice" pizza places to make 400 percent more than their competitors who sell entire pies.

MUSIC MARKETING LESSONS FROM A GAS STATION

I have a friend who owns a gas station. Once, after the price of gas had shot up, I remarked, "With gas prices going up like they are, you must be having a very good month."

His reply shocked me.

"I don't make a lot of money on gas. It's very expensive to sell. My money is made on auto service, beer, cigarettes, and candy."

People need gas for their vehicles, so he has gas available to bring them to his shop. Then he sells them the things he actually makes money on.

I suggest musicians operate their businesses in a similar way, viewing music as a way to bring people to you. This is no different from how radio works, with the exception that you may go so far as to give people copies of your music, rather than just let them listen to it.

It doesn't matter how you use music to attract people. The important thing is that you get them "in the door." Without that, you won't sell them anything.

Pay attention to this, because it's important:

You will be better off having 1,000,000 people steal your music than 10,000 people buy it.

If 1,000,000 people care about your music enough to steal it, you can find a way to monetize it. You can sell tickets to live performances and other "experiential" things that can't be copied. You can offer other music options. It doesn't matter. What matters is you have 1,000,000 people who have heard your music. That's worth something, and most acts have to pay a lot of money for it to happen.

A musician doesn't have to make a living solely from selling music. That will limit your income.

Think of music like a carnival barker, somebody who attracts the attention of people passing by and gets them to spend money elsewhere. This is much more profitable for most acts.

Because of this, a musician doesn't have to rely on selling recorded music to make a living. In the end, who cares where your income stream is coming from? What's important is that you get to make music.

Here are some examples of how the wealthiest musicians make money beyond music:

Fragrances – Justin Bieber, Rihanna, Britney Spears, Katy Perry, Lady Gaga

Clothing – Diddy, Jay-Z, Beyonce

Endorsements – Taylor Swift, Rihanna, Beyonce, Jon Bon Jovi, Dr. Dre, Toby Keith, Lil Wayne

Voice Acting – Ozzy Osbourne, Dolly Parton, Brad Paisley

Spirits – Diddy, Sammy Hagar, Toby Keith

Restaurants – Jon Bon Jovi, Jimmy Buffett, Toby Keith

While you don't have to become part owner of a hip hot dog stand or have your own eau de toilette, the power of this idea still applies to you. Let's look at the math behind what doing this can mean for you.

A gas station owner who makes money selling only gas would need tremendous volume to do well. Even if the business had that kind of volume, by not selling anything else, such as snacks, sodas, and cigarettes, the gas station owner would be leaving a lot of money on the table.

The same applies to you and recorded music.

The good news is that performing your music live can be a very powerful income stream. Even if you're playing only local or regional gigs for $10/person, you can make *a lot* of money.

An album, which a person will buy once, sells for $10. Not all of it is profit, since you have to pay for manufacturing and, unless you're selling directly, distribution fees as well.

Live shows can make you $10 (or more) for every person who attends, and many people will attend multiple shows each year. Plus, live shows offer a great opportunity to sell T-shirts and other merchandise, which will add to the money you'll make.

If you can give away music to get people through the door, multiple times per year, at $10 per person per show, is it worth it? Yes.

Music is an important part of what you do, but it's not what people are paying for, even if they purchase it. What people are paying you for is to help them feel good.

Before you can begin making the kind of money you want, you have to rise above the noise. People have to hear you before they'll become fans.

Giving away your recorded music is a surefire way to help you get heard, because it lowers the risk for potential fans. They're not out $10 for an album or even $0.99 for a single song. They get to hear your best stuff without worrying about the financial implications.

People who get your music for free, if they like it, won't abandon you. They'll pay to see your shows, buy your merch, and tell their friends about you. You'll gain new fans and make money each time this cycle of events repeats itself.

THE VALUE OF MUSIC PIRACY

There was a time when selling recorded music was a business model that most musicians could do well with. Today, because music is so easy to copy, this business model isn't as solid as it once was.

Recorded music is a beautiful thing. You do the work once and get paid again and again by selling copies of that work. Lots of people are mad that making a living this way isn't as easy as it once was. Don't be one of them.

The ease of copying music has also been a blessing for the industry. Thanks to technology like recordable CDs and the MP3 format, it's easy for people who love music to share a listening experience with others. This is free advertising that used to cost labels millions of dollars (often in the form of radio promotion). A fan who copies music for a friend is more powerful than radio advertising, though, because it comes with a personal recommendation. A recommendation from a friend is the number-one way people find out about new music.

Here is how it works:

Let's say you record a song and I really like it. I have a friend who is into similar music.

I could simply *tell* my friend about how great you are. That's a nice start, but he'd have to take my word for it.

"A picture paints 1,000 words," and a song does something similar. A better option is to let him hear it for himself.

But how?

Perhaps, if we're together, I could let him hear the song via my iPod.

Or we could wait around, listening to the radio together …

And when your song came on, I could say, "This is the song I was telling you about!"

But who is going to do that?

It's much easier (and more powerful) to be able to email a song to somebody. You can do it whenever you want, and it doesn't matter whether the other person is in your town or across the world. Beyond that, it allows the other person to listen to the music on his terms, using his equipment—not via sharing somebody else's headphones or at a random time selected by a radio programmer.

If my friend likes the song, he can listen to it multiple times. And if he really likes it, he can pass it along, starting the sharing process over again.

This is the power of being able to copy (and share) music.

IF YOU CAN'T BEAT 'EM, JOIN 'EM

"We can innovate faster than they can copy."

This is a quote by Ray Kroc, the man who turned McDonald's into the most successful fast-food operation in the world. It applies to music just as it applies to hamburgers.

Ray Kroc wasn't worried about people knocking him off. He focused on innovation and finding a better way to do things.

Music piracy, illegal downloads, file sharing, or whatever else you want to call it, is here to stay. We are not going to stop it.

What we *can* do is find a way to make it work for us.

For many musicians—maybe you—it's scary to think about somebody being able to take music without permission. It can feel like a violation.

How could people who claim to like what you do take what you've put so much blood, sweat, and tears into without paying for it? Don't they know how this affects you?

Most people don't know, because they don't understand how today's music business works. They've been told that record labels get all the money from album sales. Plus, the only images of musicians they see in the media are those of wealthy rock stars.

Regardless of how people get your music, once they have it, you have a great opportunity to build a relationship with them and convert them into paying customers. You have options for making money in the music business that go way beyond selling music and can be much more profitable. Don't trip over dollars worrying about a few pennies.

THE BIGGEST PROBLEM YOU (AND OTHER MUSICIANS) WILL FACE

Imagine that somebody has *no desire* to copy and share your music.

As a musician, that's the biggest problem you'll face. You have a much greater chance of nobody hearing your music at all than losing a significant amount of money to piracy.

So go ahead and embrace that it's good for you to have people who want to copy and share your music. You're losing an income stream (or part of one), but recorded music is a low-profit business that requires a lot of volume to make any substantial money. You'll be much better off focusing on higher-profit options, such as licensing deals, clothing, and other merchandise.

With so much negative media coverage about online music piracy, it's easy to think that simply releasing something to the public will automatically result in tens of thousands of copies of it being distributed without permission.

Not true. If you want people to spread the word about your music via copying, so you can benefit from people hearing about your music and getting excited about it, you need to encourage this behavior.

Here are four ways to do that:

- **Ask** – Don't just assume that everybody is going to share your music with friends. If you want people to spread the word about what you're doing, ask them to. Here is text you can use in liner notes for your albums or send to purchasers via a follow-up email:

  "Please pass this music to your friends and tell them about us! Email MP3 files to them, burn them CDs, or whatever you want ... It's not evil. Go ahead. Do it."

- **Let People Tape Shows** – Encouraging people to tape live shows and share the tapes with others will go a long way in getting your music into the hands of new fans and increase your connection with old fans as well.

- **Point The Way** – If you're already posting photos from each show, and you should be, go a step further by pointing people to where they can get recordings of that show. This can be done via a dedicated website or as part of an existing social media platform. Preferably, you'll do it through both.

- **Release "Unauthorized" Albums** – Release demo tapes, alternate versions, sound checks, and live recordings as "bootleg" albums to give fans the sense they're getting something special. Because most people want to be tastemakers and the nature of bootleg albums is to copy them, this material will be more likely to be passed around.

8 WAYS TO MAKE MONEY GIVING YOUR MUSIC AWAY FOR FREE

Music is a tool used to create a positive experience for your fans. It's an introduction to what is possible, much like a calling card that provides an opportunity to build a deeper relationship that goes way beyond a one-time sale.

So let's look at how to use free music to make that happen:

- **Build a Mailing List** – When you can reach people at any time, you have the power to make money. You could sell a downloadable song for $1 now, but if you trade download in exchange for contact information (phone, email, and/or postal address), you can make 100x that.

  How to do it: Use free downloads to build your mailing list and start sending offers for people to buy something!

- **Build an Audience** – A following is worth something. You'll be able to launch albums, fund Kickstarter projects, and fill venues easier when people know who you are and want to hear from you.

  How to do it: Give away music, allow people to record shows, and encourage existing fans to share your material with friends.

- **Advertising** – If you're able to reach a certain demographic, there are companies that will pay to ride along with you through the form of advertising.

  How to do it: Become a "partner" on YouTube, put Google Adsense on your site, or sell the opportunity for a company to sponsor a free show.

- **A "Free" License** – Give away use of your music in exchange for exposure, a future paid licensing deal, or advertising.

How to do it: Approach film school students, filmmakers on Kickstarter, and YouTube vloggers with the opportunity to use you music free in exchange for links, first right of refusal on a paid licensing deal (should the show/film get picked up), or exposure to help you build an audience.

- **Sell What Can't Be Copied** – Give away music free and sell what can't be copied, like a live show or personal appearances.

  How to do it: Give away your music, and encourage others to do the same, in order to build an audience. Make money selling what can't be copied, like a live show or personal appearances.

- **Special Editions** – Give away the "basic" version free and sell specially packaged, "collectible" editions.

  How to do it: When you release an album, make three versions—a free version (download), a standard version (CD/vinyl), and a "collectible" version, with something people highly value, such as a personalized message and autograph, handwritten lyrics or one-of-a-kind artwork.

- **Drugs and Chick-fil-A** – Drug companies make billions providing doctors free samples to give to patients, because once you try something that works, you'll pay to get more of it. Fast food restaurant Chick-fil-A provides free samples of its chicken, because people who like it enough will buy an entire meal.

  How to do it: Give away your best song and charge people for the full album.

- **The Value of Being Everywhere** – Tens of millions of people use pirated copies of Microsoft Windows. The number is about 1/3 of all users. Still, being everywhere has value for Microsoft when it comes to selling auxiliary services, such as virus protection.

  How to do it: Give away music, allow people to record shows, and encourage existing fans to share your material with friends. Make money on things that can't be copied, such as live shows and events. Add income streams not affected by piracy.

CONCLUSION

The greatest threat you face as a musician is that nobody will ever hear your music. If enough people hear you, there are opportunities for you to make money.

Do whatever you can to unleash your music, even if it means giving it away free or encouraging others to copy it. The attention you'll get, the fans you'll gain, and the money you'll earn in other ways will be worth it.

CHAPTER 8:

FIND YOUR BALANCE

What do you *really* want out of your music business?

Do you want to be known around the country? Around the world?

Do you want to hear your music on the radio? See yourself on television?

Focus on what you want and know *why* you want it.

It's OK to "think big," and I encourage you to do so, but realize that sometimes it's the small things that will have the biggest impact on you.

For example, there are very few things that will change your life (and give momentum to your music career) like selling your first 10,000 albums. The money and other benefits you'll get from selling 10,000 albums are enough for most artists to do music full time. If you're currently working a day job, this is life changing. Not only will you have enough money to live on, you'll also have more time to devote to writing, recording, and performing.

Once you get clear on your goals, it will completely change how you're able to approach things and open you up to new opportunities for success.

Consider these questions when creating your music business goals:

- How do I want to live?

- How do I want to impact the people who hear my music?

- Do I want a life outside of music?

- What am I willing to do in exchange for success in the music business?

- Are there any other career options that would make me happy?

- What activities does my "dream day" consist of?

Focus on what you want at this moment, knowing that you can always revise your list at any time. Your goals can change and will change, because you'll change during your process of going after them.

WHAT ARE YOUR MUSIC BUSINESS GOALS?

Everybody has goals, or at least *thinks* they have goals. Only a handful of people are actually making an active effort to get clarity on what they really want and then go after those things in a deliberate way.

Beyond that, many people have goals that focus only on money and popularity. While these are two topics you should absolutely be thinking about, a look at the bigger picture is more likely to ensure other important areas of your life are not neglected.

Happiness

Martin Seligman, an American psychologist, found that humans seem happiest when they have:

- Pleasure (tasty foods, warm baths, etc.);

- Engagement (also known as "flow," this is what happens when you are absorbed in and enjoying an activity);

- Relationships (social connections);

- Meaning (being part of something bigger than yourself); and

- Accomplishments (the realization of having specific and measureable goals).

Here is another that I'd add to the list:

- Autonomy (freedom and control)

Stephen Covey, in his book *The 7 Habits of Highly Effective People*, said, "Every public victory is preceded by a private victory."

This is important to remember as you go about achieving your music business goals. To make something happen externally, you will need to accomplish things internally.

Similarly, what the music business looks like from the outside is often very different from what the music business looks like from the inside. Things are not always as they appear. If you've ever wondered why somebody will suddenly leave an A-List band, touring arenas around the world and selling millions of albums, to start his own, much smaller project, or even retire from the business completely, remember this.

This is your career being sculpted, so set it up any way you want. The generic music business goals, such as selling tons of music and playing for big crowds, while they may be OK for some, don't necessarily have to be what you choose. If you'd rather give away your music and stick with small, intimate venues, do it.

Happiness starts now, right where you are. If you're not happy creating music with the equipment you currently have, it's unlikely you'll suddenly be happy with different equipment. New equipment (just like bigger crowds and more money) can add to an experience, but it's not the spark that ignites it.

While touring is an important part of music promotion and a great income stream, you don't have to constantly be on the road. There are plenty of acts that only play on the weekends or tour just in the summer. This will help you to have some semblance of order and stability, which can be important for maintaining friendships and other social connections. Touring and playing live shows is, in my opinion, still the very best way for musicians to connect with fans and make money while doing it, but if that doesn't work for you, find something you do enjoy that will give you similar results.

If you're playing in an already-established band and what you're doing is no longer fulfilling, a side project may give you the creative freedom you're looking for. You'll have income from your main project but the freedom and control of doing whatever you want elsewhere.

Regardless of your current circumstances or preferences, there are ways to make money in the music business. For example, it's not common, but also not unheard of, to find musicians on YouTube who make a full-time income via its revenue-sharing plan, simply by recording and uploading videos.

Nashville-based musician Geoff Smith, in addition to a career as an artist, jumped in on the multimillion-dollar ringtone market with RingtoneFeeder.com, a service that sends subscribers custom ringtones each week for a monthly fee.

Dave Stringer combined a love of meditation, neuroscience, and music to create a unique and interactive performance that has taken him around the globe. His recorded music is played at yoga studios worldwide and has appeared on numerous film soundtracks, including the third film in the *Matrix* trilogy, *Matrix Revolutions*.

Billy Grisack, known professionally as Mister Billy, started a career in writing and performing music for children after visiting his son's kindergarten class. He co-wrote the "I'm a Big Kid Now" jingle used by Huggies Pull-Ups and does over 200 shows each year at schools, libraries, and festivals. He has been making his living as a musician for over 30 years.

You have options when it comes to music business success.

Get clear on what will make you happy, and build your career around that. This will allow you to get the results you want while still enjoying the process.

Popularity

For some people, popularity is defined by being able to tour full time, bringing in enough people to fill big venues, or sell enough music to chart on Billboard. Others want to be in magazines, be interviewed on Oprah-style talk shows, or be followed by photographers everywhere they go.

What does "popularity" mean to you?

You may have heard the joke about an unknown band being "big in Japan." Today, a variation on that joke is to say an act is "big on the Internet."

But it's not really a joke … It's rare, but not totally unheard of for musicians who never tour or even play live to have 100,000+ subscribers on YouTube with videos that get thousands (or even millions) of hits.

Jeffree Star started his music career on Myspace, with his songs receiving over 100,000,000 plays. His self-released debut album, *Plastic Surgery Slumber Party*, was number one on the iTunes dance music chart. Since then, he's toured the world; appeared in several music videos by several major label artists, including Good Charlotte, Ke$ha, and Amy Winehouse; and signed his own major-label deal.

Not exactly a household name, but certainly a guy with a level of popularity and success that many musicians would envy.

Jeffree Star was in the right place at the right time but was able to take advantage of opportunity. He was already popular online prior to Myspace, but when Myspace took off, he convinced his fans to follow him there, which gave him an early advantage as one of the most connected people on the site.

It's easy to think that opportunities like what happened to Jeffree Star no longer exist, but with so many new music and social media sites being developed, the opportunities available to you are greater than ever. You simply have to know how to take advantage of them.

The good thing about building a solid following is that it works today, just like it worked yesterday, just like it will work tomorrow. It always works.

If you're interested in being popular, start with where you are now. Focus on building your fan base one person at a time and keeping in touch with the people who are already fans.

The best type of exposure, which is not affected by trends in media and will never go away, is word of mouth. If you can encourage your fans to say good things about you, you will *always* have a career.

It's the connections you make with fans during the early stages of your career, when you have *hundreds* of fans and are able to go above and beyond what you'll be able to do when you have *thousands* of fans (or more), that will provide the solid foundation you need to stick around the music business for as long as you want.

A great example of how to do this is making contact with fans after they've purchased your music, because this turns a one-way interaction (them buying something from you) into a two-way conversation. A simple note in a package you're sending or post on Facebook are quick and easy ways to reach out, establish better connection, and let the people who support you know they are valued.

Slow and steady wins the race. Even if you have so many fans that you can't possibly reach out to all of them in a personal way, make the effort to at least reach out to *some* on a frequent basis. It will be time well spent.

Popularity varies. You don't have to be as big as you may think before you are doing well in the music business. Shows like *American Idol* have skewed many people into believing a career in the music business is an all-or-nothing thing, with aspiring musicians transforming into household names overnight. However, overnight successes are rare. The majority of well-known acts have built their careers, just as I've suggested you do, slow and steady.

Don't wait for success to come to you. You can start building it right now.

Respect and Admiration

The ultimate sign of respect and admiration is when people give you their money in exchange for your product or service.

While it's nice to get positive, professional acclaim from people within the industry, most of the time, those people are not the ones you're making music for.

Some musicians *do* care about keeping critics and music industry executives happy. If this is you, that's fine. Playing to critics and others within the industry is neither good nor bad; it's just a different audience. So if having the industry love you or getting a "5-Star" write-up in a major music magazine is important to you, there is nothing wrong with that.

Music critics are often looking for something completely different than people at record labels are. Music critics want to be tastemakers.

Record labels are more concerned about how well an album sells than anything else. Record labels would sign an act of mimes if audio recordings of silence would sell.

It's fine to want the respect and admiration from people within the industry, whether they are critics, record label staff, or anybody else.

Don't think you need any of this in order to be successful with fans, though.

Fans care about one thing—feeling good. What critics think doesn't matter. What label you're on doesn't matter.

You've probably heard the saying, "To get respect, you have to give it." Never has this been truer than within the music industry.

People know what's real and authentic. We have a sixth sense—a BS detector that alerts us when something isn't genuine.

The best way to start building respect within the music industry is to get it from your own people. For example, if you're a Christian artist, you want respect from people within the Christian community. If you don't have it there, you won't get it anywhere.

And how do you get respect from people? Again, "to get respect, you have to give it."

This means not being careless with your audience.

People who buy your music, come to your shows, and otherwise support you are investing time, money, and attention to do so. They want to be entertained and have an experience that leaves them feeling good.

You *must* show up prepared. This means not only doing the needed work, like knowing how to put on a good show, but also taking the time to understand who your audience is and what they expect from musicians they like.

You *must* give them value and live up to their expectations. If you don't, and they feel cheated, they'll leave.

Beyond expected value, do what you can to over-deliver. It's rare to find people who do more than they're asked, so if you can, you'll stand out from the crowd.

In the end, getting respect and admiration from fans comes down to these two things:

- Understanding how your audience is experiencing you currently

- Understanding how your audience wants to experience you and giving them that experience (and more)

Security

Beyond the very basic needs of the ability to breathe, food, water, and shelter, "security" (or safety) is something to consider when planning your music business career.

Security and safety needs include:

- financial security

- emotional security

- health and well-being

The desire for security is one of our most powerful drivers. Because of this, it can hinder us from taking risks, such as those in the music business. Beyond that, feeling lack of security in your life will affect your ability to create. How can you get into the emotional place needed to write a great song when you're worried about how you're going to pay your bills?

"Security" differs from person to person. I once knew a guy who wanted "three years of savings" in the bank before he would quit his job. I met a musician who was making more money with his music than he was at his job but still didn't quit to go full time.

On the other hand, I've seen guys with less than $1,000 in the bank quit their jobs to pursue music and never go back. Everyone was terrified but found a previously unknown strength and desire to succeed after deciding to move forward without a backup plan.

And we've all seen wealthy people who are terrified of losing it all ...

Security is not black and white. Neither is there a perfect moment to go full time with music.

There was a time when people thought the epitome of security was a job at an established company, but we all know, even those with union-organized jobs can get laid off unexpectedly all the time. And how many "until death do us part" married couples end up in divorce court?

The only security you have is within you. It comes when you trust yourself, and trust your ability to handle things when it's time to take needed action.

As long as you have the ability to take action, you're secure. This is why people with less than $1,000 in the bank can quit their jobs and move forward: they know any problems that come up will only be temporary.

What do you need to feel secure? It's not a job or money or somebody else—it's something within you.

If you're looking to transition to doing music full time or are already full time and struggling with feeling secure, I urge you to look at *internal* elements of yourself rather than focusing on external things, such as a house, a car, or your bank balance.

When you feel secure internally, you will have what you need to get all your external needs met and more.

If you could walk into a recording studio, look at the chart once, and nail your part in a single take, would that help you feel secure?

If you could write a hit song, again and again, would that help you feel secure?

If you could get a last-minute call to entertain a crowd, by yourself, for four hours, would that help you feel secure?

Whatever skills you need to feel confident with your ability to provide for yourself, do what it takes to attain them.

ARE YOU MOVING CLOSER TO YOUR GOALS?

Once you have a list of things you want to accomplish, before you do anything, ask yourself this question ...

"Is what I'm about to do getting me closer to my goal of _____?"

If the answer is yes, take action. If not, and you're frustrated that you're not accomplishing your goals fast enough, find something else that will help you to get where you want to go.

Focus on activities that get you tangible results in the form of selling more music, getting more people to your shows, or otherwise bringing in money. Not what *might* sell more music, what *might* get more people to shows, or *might* make you money.

Let's be honest: in this context, "might" = probably not.

Sure, it's completely possible that you "might" get a record deal and become an internationally known pop star from sending your demo to 1,000 addresses you find in a music magazine—but it's not likely.

And it's completely possible that it "might" help your record sales if you release a sex tape—but it's not likely.

Here are some activities to avoid:

- putting flyers on cars

- randomly adding "friends" to the latest social media site

- walking up to strangers and expecting them to care about your music

- sending an email about your gig in NYC to somebody who's in LA

- wrapping your car with a photo of yourself and your new album

While these things may make you feel like you're doing work, you're not. In fact, if you're doing things like this, it may actually be dragging down the work you actually are doing.

Don't pretend to be in the music business by doing busywork. Evaluate what you're spending your time, money, and energy on and be honest with yourself as to the results you're getting.

THE 80/20 RULE

The Pareto principle, commonly known as the 80/20 rule, states that, for many events, roughly 80 percent of the results come from 20 percent of the actions.

This 80/20 rule can be found throughout your music business. For example:

- 80 percent of your gig income comes from 20 percent of the gigs you play.

- 80 percent of the money you make comes from 20 percent of your fans.

- 80 percent of recorded music sales come from 20 percent of your albums.

- 80 percent of your publishing income comes from 20 percent of your songs.

The big takeaway here is that not everything you do is getting equal results for you. If you can find the 20 percent of things that are getting you the most results, and then focus the time you have on doing more of that activity, you'll see a huge increase in your music business success.

Let's assume you measure your success by the amount of money you bring in ...

If you currently earn 80 percent of your income from live gigs, but spend only 20 percent of your time playing live gigs, you need to replace the low-level activities you are currently spending the remaining 80 percent of your time on with more live gigs. You could increase your income by as much as 400 percent by doing so.

Here is a list of other high-level activities that work well when it comes to selling music, bringing people to your shows, and making money:

- **Playing a Gig** – This is the best way to expose a lot of people to your music at once, because it affects all of their senses and there is an automatic element of social proof. In addition, you will get paid via ticket sales, merch sales, or album sales.

- **Partnering with Successful Bands** – This lets you leverage the audience and credibility of other, already successful bands, which will shortcut your time to build your own audience and credibility.

- **Building a Mailing List** – This lets you contact your fans at any time, to deepen your relationships with them or inform them of money-making ventures, such as new music for sale and upcoming live shows.

- **Giving Away Your Music** – People will consume it (and later want more of it, which you'll sell them).

- **Licensing Your Music** (for film and television) – You'll reach new people with your music, as well as getting paid for its use.

- **Licensing Your Logo/Image** – This will expose you in a different, non-musical way to both new and current fans, as well as make you money.

- **Taping Every Live Show** – You can sell recordings of your performances immediately after every show, use them to build a mailing list, or simply build rapport with fans (and get them talking about you) by letting them trade the recordings with other fans.

Nobody is perfect, and no musician is going to be 100 percent effective when it comes to doing activities that get results. However, by thinking about what you're doing (before you do it) and actually being aware of how you're spending your time, you'll get a lot more done than your competition and have a much greater chance of meeting your goals.

Even if money isn't your main goal for doing music, I suggest you have at least a secondary goal involving money, because it will give you something measurable to track. Fans vote with their wallets, and measurement eliminates argument, so this will enable you to see how well you're really doing as opposed to how well you think you're doing.

THE BALANCE OF BUSINESS AND ART

Creating music is a very different skill from the business topics discussed in this book, but it is no less important on the list of activities that will make you money. Everything in this book is based on a quality song.

You need both art and business to succeed in this industry. Without a good song to build your music business on, you have no real business. However, you could have the best song in the world, and if nobody ever heard it, it wouldn't matter.

Creating a great song requires you to use a different area of your brain than other aspects of your music business require, such as booking shows, negotiating contracts, or planning a marketing strategy. The good news is that your ability to easily switch from your "business" mind to your "creative" mind will improve with practice.

Here are ways to help make this happen ...

Write Daily

Like playing your instrument, your ability to write well will improve with focused and dedicated practice. I suggest scheduling time to write daily, as opposed to falling into the trap of waiting for inspiration.

Inspiration is all around you. Writing daily will help you tap into it.

Have a Writing Ritual

It can help if you have a routine to help you focus on being creative. This can be as simple as taking a few minutes to sit quietly or using that time to look through the newspaper, picking out writing prompts.

The important thing here is not what you do, but giving yourself a finite amount of time to do it in. This is not a time to delay the work you have to do or otherwise add to the resistance you may already feel; it's the "on-ramp" to that part of the brain you'll use to come up with great material.

Keep reading to learn more about something called the Pomodoro Technique. Not only can you use it to help get business tasks done, but you can also use it when you are writing songs.

Have a Designated Writing Space

The ability for your brain to focus on "creativity" rather than other things, such as your relationship (or lack thereof), your health, or paying your bills, will be helped when you have a specific place used only for your creative pursuits. For some, this is a specific room of the house that isn't used for other activities, such as eating or watching television. For others, it will be a local coffee shop that you go to only when you want to write. This will let your mind know, "I'm here in my creative space, so now it's time to get to work."

Putting these things in place will help you become more creative as well as get into a creative mindset more easily. You'll be able to create better art more quickly, which will help you better keep your fans engaged— and make more money.

TAKING CARE OF BUSINESS

If you wanted to do *more* business, you would have chosen a career on the business end of the industry rather than the creative. Still, if you want to make money with your music, there are some business aspects of the industry that you won't be able to completely get away from.

There are three types of business tasks:

- tasks you like to do

- tasks you *don't* like to do

- tasks only you can do

Before you start to categorize tasks and activities into these three areas, it's important that you disregard old thoughts on what you feel you should and shouldn't enjoy. Being honest with yourself about the things you like and *don't* like doing will help you get more done in less time, but perhaps more importantly, actually enjoy the process.

To find out if you *really* like doing something, ask yourself the following question:

"If money, judgement from others, and needed resources to successfully complete this task were not issues, would I still be doing it?"

If the answer is yes, and you can do it without neglecting anything else in your business, go for it.

When it comes to doing the tasks you don't like doing, look at options that will enable you to either have somebody else do them or eliminate them entirely. Life is too short to do a lot of things you don't enjoy.

With that said, if you're getting started in the music business and have limited resources with which to outsource tasks, you may benefit from experiencing parts of the business that you don't enjoy. The firsthand knowledge about the various parts of the business you'll learn will help you better create a system in which to hand things over to somebody else.

Firsthand knowledge of different aspects of your business is always helpful. Many top music business executives started their careers in the mailroom, worked their ways through the ranks, and are successful for this very reason. Today, companies like Zappos.com and UPS do this on purpose, training their executives by starting them in nonexecutive positions, such as answering phones or delivering packages.

As a musician, there are certain tasks only you can do. They include things like live performances; personal appearances such as "meet and greet" events, interviews, and media; and anything having to do with product creation (such as writing and recording). These things are more optional than you might imagine, though, and it should be noted that there have been many successful acts to break these rules, avoiding interviews, refusing personal appearances, and having material written by other people and recorded by studio musicians.

While it's possible to outsource *most* music business tasks, there are some things you should handle personally. The music business is highly personality driven, and things like personal appearances and interviews will help you stand out from the competition and make your career pop.

Regardless of whether you're doing tasks yourself or have somebody else who does them for you, here are four final thoughts that will help you get more done with the resources you have:

- **Have a Goal** – Decide your destination and then go there. Get clear on what you want to accomplish and work from a list of small tasks that will help you get there. This will help you keep focused on what you're doing and why you're doing it.

- **Take the Bitter Pill First** – Knock out the most unpleasant task first, instead of delaying it until later or ignoring it, hoping it will go away. This will free up energy and make everything afterward seem easy by comparison.

- **Bundle Up** – Do similar tasks, like phone calls, in a single group. Think of this like you would approach shopping at a mall. You wouldn't go to the mall to shop at one store, then go home, then make another trip to the mall later. Whether you're in the same mental space or physical space, take care of everything in that area in one shot.

- **Handle It Once** – Once you start a task, work until it's complete. If something comes up during your work, put it on your to-do list and deal with it later. Completed tasks make you money, while incomplete tasks drain your time and energy.

The bottom line when it comes to your music business is that when something needs to be done, like it or not, it's your responsibility to make sure it happens. You don't want to be the best songwriter or musician the world has never heard of. Do everything you can to get the word out about your music. Anything less isn't respecting your art and creative talent.

HOW TO SEGMENT YOUR WORK

No matter what your circumstances, between bringing in money (however you do that), creating music, rehearsing, maintaining relationships, and taking care of your own emotional and physical needs, you have limited time to devote to music business tasks. However, the hard reality is that, to have a successful music career, you *must* find a way to take care of these tasks. Because of this, you need to make the most of your time.

If you're properly utilizing your time, it's very possible to get all of your music business work done. Even if your time is extremely limited due to a day job or other obligations, come up with an amount of time that you'll be able to consistently devote to doing this work. Short, consistent work sessions are more effective and will allow you to get more done than longer, disrupted work sessions.

Determine how much time you have, map out a schedule, and start doing the necessary tasks to build your music business. Don't wait for a perfect situation (such as until after you've quit your day job) to get going. Start where you are right now.

Here are the four categories you should be focusing your time on. Alternate between these categories, even if you have limited time, to make sure you do the needed work for each one:

- **Communication** – You should spend at least an hour per day sending personal messages to fans, as well as establishing (and keeping alive) contacts within the industry.

- **Creating Income** – This is defined as activity leading to something that you'll *directly* earn money from. Potential to earn money doesn't count here. Examples include booking gigs that pay you money, negotiating endorsements, and leasing equipment that you own to other bands.

- **Creating Content** – Writing songs, recording songs, and making videos for YouTube fall into this category. "Content" is anything you can sell, such as albums, as well as anything you can use to promote yourself, such as a video tour diary.

- **Looking for Opportunity** – Time you spend looking for new opportunities goes in this category. This is where you will discover new ways to generate income, expand your territory, or build a deeper connection with fans.

Don't let perceived lack of time keep you from getting important tasks done. You probably have more time than you realize. For most of us, the reason it seems like we have so little time has less to do with being truly busy and has a lot to do with the biggest enemy of getting things done: distraction.

The only time you need to be around people while working is if they're essential to the task you're working on. If you work from home, let other members of your household know that you are not to be interrupted when working.

Obviously, tools such as phones and computers can be as much help to your music business as they are a distraction. These require special handling when working on tasks where they are needed. If you need to make phone calls for business, such as booking gigs, do it. Don't let phone calls and text messages distract you from other work, though. If you keep interrupting what you're doing to answer a call or read a text message every time one comes in, you'll never complete anything.

While computers are helpful for communicating with fans or music industry people, you're one click away from being distracted. When using a computer for business, stick with that task. If you find yourself unable to do this, there are several programs and browser plug-ins available that will block access to email, websites, and social media for a set period of time.

YOUR KEY TO GETTING THINGS DONE – A TIMER

One of the most effective ways to ensure you get everything done in the time you have is to use the Pomodoro Technique. It's a time management method developed by Francesco Cirillo that uses a timer to break down periods of work into 25-minute intervals separated by breaks.

The method is based on the idea that frequent breaks can improve mental agility.

There are five basic steps to implementing the technique:

1. Decide on the task to be done.

2. Set the timer to 25 minutes.

3. Work on the task until the timer rings; record with an X.

4. Take a short break (five minutes).

5. Every four 25-minute intervals, take a longer break (15–20 minutes).

Get a kitchen timer, rather than using the built-in timer on your phone or computer. Again, the purpose of this is to eliminate distraction. Having a specific device for this also tells your brain that it's time to work.

As a working musician, you will be pulled in many different directions. While you won't be able to totally eliminate distraction, you *can* successfully manage it.

The Pomodoro Technique works, but like any time management technique, it's not a magic pill. Consistency in its use is what will make it work for you.

IF YOU WANT SOMETHING DONE RIGHT ...

Time is our most precious commodity. The only ways to work around the limit of time are to work more effectively yourself or leverage the time of others in order to get your tasks done.

The common saying of "if you want something done right, do it yourself" is false. This is perhaps the number-one reason people don't delegate tasks, but the truth is, there are plenty of people who can do *most* of what you are doing, and they may be able to do it faster and better than you do.

Your fans want to be in the music business with you. Don't wait around for them to show up and start working without being asked. Ask people for help, and they will help you.

Here are a few core principles to remember when it comes to leading people:

- **Be Specific** – If you want something done in a certain way, you need to be very specific with your instructions. While this may seen "authoritarian" at first, the majority of people working for you (including volunteers) will prefer that you tell them exactly what you want (as opposed to giving little or no specifics about the job), since it won't require them to make as many important decisions about how things should be done.

- **Be Patient** – People will mess things up. This is how we learn what not to do. Forgive mistakes and move on.

- **Have a Backup Plan** – Be ready to call in other people, do something else, or jump in yourself, should something fail. Don't let anything somebody else does keep you from attaining your goal.

- **Recognize and Praise** – Take care of your people. If somebody does a good job, let him know.

There are several ways to be a great leader. If you hold your vision, stay open to feedback, and learn from your mistakes, the experience will be a positive one for both you and the people you work with.

HOW TO AVOID BURNOUT

Taking your music business career to the level you want is going to require dedicated effort. The sheer amount of work and time you devote to your career, not to mention the many tasks you juggle, can seem overwhelming at times. It's important to set a pace that will allow you to achieve your goals, but not at the expense of your mental or physical health.

Acknowledge Little Victories

If you're working from a list, simply crossing off a task may be the only acknowledgement you need to move forward to the next. As your goals and what it takes to achieve them get larger, though, you may want to do something more for yourself, as this will help you to keep both focused on the end result as well as motivated to see it through.

Stopping to acknowledge little successes you have will help you to enjoy the process, which is often overlooked with so much focus on attainment of goals. For example, if somebody emails to say he loves your music, don't just write it off or take it for granted. Having people love your music is what you're in this business for, so take time to acknowledge any success you have with this, even if it's just to yourself.

Prioritize

Keep in mind the outcome you're looking for and know why each task you're involved with is important.

If something comes up while you're working, don't add it to that day's list. There are *always* important things to take care of, and adding more to your current day's workload will increase your chance of burnout. Instead, add all nonemergency business to tomorrow's list of important activities.

Decline all nonessential tasks. The best way to avoid being overburdened with work is to not have that work in the first place. Focus on opportunities that fit into your marketing plan. For example, play the show in the town you're trying to break, but don't bother with an opportunity to play 1,500 miles away in a town you'll probably never visit again. This is a business, and you're not that desperate for a gig.

Have a Daily "Reset" Switch

During your workday, have a "reset" switch to keep your mind (and body) fresh and engaged. This could be a walk around the block, time in a rocking chair, or a gym workout. It doesn't matter what you do to reset, as long as it works.

A reset will help you reduce stress, keep you mentally healthy, and is great for getting "alone time" to work through both business and personal problems. It will also train your brain to switch from "business" to "non-business" modes more quickly, allowing you to write songs and handle other creative aspects of your business with greater ease.

Disconnect

You should set aside time each week to completely disconnect from your work. This should be something *beyond* your daily reset.

Have an evening, or even an entire day, with no business, no phone, no email, and no online access. Many professional writers and songwriters have "writing cabins" and other off-the-grid locations where they're able to eliminate common distractions and completely focus on creative endeavors or just get away.

While this may sound counterintuitive to you, disconnecting for a while will actually help you get more done in the time you are working, because you'll be refreshed and ready to hit the ground running when you return back to work.

You want a career you can maintain over a period of years, not months. Pace yourself. You'll get more done by taking a slow and steady approach, improving on your skills (and situation) every day, rather than an inconsistent, "stop, go fast, stop" way of doing things.

CONCLUSION

Keep this in mind when you're working on new material or otherwise working on a goal. Everybody who has ever done anything great has been right there with you in terms of dealing with distraction. Beyond that, everybody who has ever done something great has had to deal with resistance, most of which comes from the person they see when looking in the mirror.

Get clear on your goals, and do whatever it takes to get them done. That is the difference between an amateur and a professional.

CHAPTER 9:

BE FLEXIBLE AND KEEP MOVING FORWARD

The saying "if you keep doing what you're doing, you'll keep getting what you're getting" is true in a lot of cases. This is not true in the music business.

The music business is in constant change. Because of this, those who haven't changed along with it have been left behind.

THE MOVIE MAN

I know a guy who had a video rental business. From 1985 until 1999, he was making money hand over fist. However, even then, his business was dying.

The DVD player was the fastest-selling piece of home electronics ever. Because of this, the video rental business changed within a very short period of time. However, the Movie Man, because he was in a small town with people who didn't seem to have the desire to upgrade, had a little more time than most before he was affected by the change.

But people did upgrade ... eventually. So he did also. Fortunately, it was an easy transition. The only thing he had to do was replace the videotapes on his shelves with DVDs.

189

Then DVD-by-mail services, like Netflix, came along. They had a much bigger selection of movies and charged less than brick-and-mortar stores.

He lost a few customers, but very few of his customers had computers, so he lucked out—for a while. As more and more people started to get computers, he lost more and more customers.

But he had one thing that Netflix and the major stores didn't: porn. And his tiny "Adults Only" room in the back corner kept the rest of the store in business—until his customers discovered the Internet was full of porn and it was a lot less awkward to get titles like "3D House of Boobs" online than from him.

Then Redbox and other automated kiosk services came to town. How do you compete with a service that costs as little as $1, has more locations than you do, and never closes?

His solution was to use fear, telling people that those who used Redbox were at risk for identity theft. Most people aren't idiots, though, and a lot of the ones who are will take convenience over risk, so he lost to Redbox anyway.

In the end, he was bringing in maybe $200 on a good night. Sure, there were people who were still interested in coming to a physical store for their movie rentals, but there wasn't enough money coming in to keep the lights on, employees paid, and the racks filled with the latest releases.

DOES THIS SOUND LIKE YOU?

You may be extremely skilled at marketing or working within a genre or market that hasn't been as affected by a switch from CDs to downloads or piracy or whatever else is affecting everybody else. You will be affected eventually, though.

It's easy to look at a situation after the fact, when the transition is over and you have all the facts, and then criticize from a position of hindsight. When you're in the middle of a situation while it's happening, your view of things is completely different.

Changes in the market, even "big" things like those mentioned above, can seem subtle when you're in the middle of running your businesses. And it can be easy to think, "my customers are different" or "my business is different." Neither your customers nor your business is immune to change, though. If you're not moving forward, you'll eventually be left with nothing.

This isn't something to be scared of; just be aware. Had the Movie Man been paying attention to the shift in his industry, he could have sold his retail store and gotten in on the automated kiosk business. Instead of the situation that ultimately put him out of business, he likely would have been making more money than ever.

The same thing applies to you. Sometimes the thing that can crush you will be your biggest opportunity for growth.

The music business is constantly changing in terms of how music is distributed and money is made. The way we consume music these days is completely different from how we consumed it even just a few years ago.

There will be opportunities to make money that we can't even dream about now, because the ways we'll do it don't yet exist. Some of the things that are working now either won't work as well or won't work at all.

Also, the world will continue to be filled with more and more noise. Even today, anybody can make a song, put it online, and have worldwide distribution. The same thing can be done with videos, books, and any other form of entertainment. Imagine what that will be like in just a few years.

People are getting bombarded with messages, from the time they wake up to the time they go to bed at night. And because of this, we're getting more and more immune to them.

There was a time when being on *The Tonight Show* would cause your career to skyrocket. Because there were not a lot of entertainment options, millions of people would tune in nightly.

Those days are over. *The Tonight Show* audience has been split thousands of different ways, thanks to video games, texting, cheap long-distance calls, online video, pay-per-video movies, video rental, 100+ cable or satellite television channels, online message boards, audio books, 24-hour gyms, and who knows what else. And now that marketing people know we like options, our choices will only continue to expand.

This is why top music business acts, the ones that can get attention, are making more money than ever. If Katy Perry has proved she can attract attention enough to sell a lot of records, why not expand on that by putting her in a movie, releasing a perfume named after her, or having her promote a new brand of soda?

And the opposite is true as well: if Kim Kardashian can get an audience for a sex tape or reality television show, why not make a record and give that audience more to enjoy?

This is where "noise" at the bottom level works to your advantage in a big way. Once you can break away from the pack, you no longer have to compete with other musicians there. And because those left behind are likely to drown each other out and never break away themselves, your future competition is limited as well.

How do you break away from the pack? Play your game.

FORGET THE FORMAT AND DISTRIBUTION

Like the Movie Man above, if you get too connected to one way of doing business, one distribution method, or one income stream, you'll likely die with it. In order to have any longevity in this business, you must be light on your feet and willing to change your approach when needed.

The format on which we sell music doesn't matter, because the way we distribute music is changing. This isn't new and isn't temporary: it's always been the case and always will be.

Don't get attached to CDs, MP3s, or vinyl, just like you're not attached to cassettes, 8-tracks, MiniDiscs, DCCs, DATs, or phonograph cylinders. All formats, even current ones, will eventually die to make room for something else, and you don't want your music to die with them.

On the same note, don't get attached to iTunes or Amazon for distribution, just like you're not attached to Sam Goody, Record Bar, Tower Records, or Sam the Record Man. Distribution options die too.

Both music format and music distribution are moving targets that constantly change. When releasing music, focus on the best way to get it to fans at that time. If you don't know what that is, ask them.

Both the music format you sell and where you sell it will change. How we'll do things in five years probably hasn't been invented yet, so don't worry about figuring out the exact details.

Focus on the music itself. If you have that in order, the rest will work out.

FORGET THE WEBSITE

Where people go to find music online is changing. Where people go to find bands is changing. In 1995, IUMA was popular. Then MP3. com came along. Since then, Myspace was once the "go-to" destination. Facebook has been popular. And there are dozens of others ...

None of them really matter in the grand scheme of things. And all of them will die sooner than your music act should.

Should you have a presence on the current popular online music sites? Absolutely. But don't get caught up in thinking any of them will be the solution to your music business problems.

Being on a popular music site is great, because some fans will find out about you that way. Most people go to music sites looking for something very specific, though: they are not "browsing" random music, looking for something new.

The majority of people will find out about what you're doing not through websites, but recommendations by their friends. These endorsements of you will set the stage for the connection and rapport you're looking to build. It's up to you to build upon that, though.

Here is how to do it:

    1. Play live shows.

    2. Follow up with people you meet and have a "conversation" with them.

That's it. Not as sexy as Facebook or Twitter or whatever the latest online trend is, but it gets the job done in a way that nothing online can.

The only reason you should do anything online is to back up what you are doing offline.

THE HARSH REALITY OF THE MUSIC BUSINESS (AND HOW TO NAVIGATE IT)

You've been reading this book for a while, so I'm going to assume that, at this point, you're going to finish things out and go for it —whatever "going for it" means to you. I think of myself as a pretty pragmatic person, giving both the positives and negatives of things, but in my heart, I'm an optimist—I know that doing well in the music business is possible, because I see it daily. And I know you can do it.

I hope that, as you've read through the chapters, you too see that it's possible for you to do well in the music business. I believe there is plenty of room here and that a seat at the table is always available if you want one.

With that said, the one thing I absolutely don't want to do, or even be accused of, is blowing smoke up your ass. The reality is, as possible as it is for you to do well in the music business, there are some obstacles you're going to have to overcome before you can do so.

The good news is the same as the bad news: the major obstacle in the way of your music business success is you.

While it sounds easy to get out of your own way and let good things happen, from my experience, both personally and from working with hundreds of other music business people, that rarely happens at first. The physical work is easy, but getting to the point where you're mentally ready to be successful is usually much more challenging than it appears.

Below are some common challenges I've seen up-and-coming musicians face over the years and how I suggest dealing with them ...

No Money

You're building your career but not bringing in enough money to do it the way you want.

This is probably the most common problem for up-and-coming musicians. It's especially tough for solo artists who need to pay backing musicians for rehearsals, recording, and performances.

Even if you're in a partnership with other band members, this can affect you simply due to the economics of travel. In short, it's more expensive to get transportation, food, and housing for multiple people than it is for one.

Obviously, there are a lot of ways to finance things, including day jobs, loans, and trust funds. But day jobs keep you away from your music, loans have to be paid back, and most people don't have trust funds, so the best option for musicians who are short on money is to simply work more.

If you're a solo artist who plays with a backing band or if you're the front person in a band, a solo performance with just you accompanying yourself with either piano or guitar is a good option. It will get you into venues you can't play as a full band, it's less expensive to make happen, and you'll keep fans engaged (and paying you money).

Look at other music-business-related work, including backing other acts live or in the studio. Performing in other situations, such as a tribute band or cover band, is also an option.

Think beyond "I can't ..." Instead, think "What if ..." Then start thinking of possibilities to make what you want happen.

For example, what if you could partner with other musicians to share the cost of a tour—share equipment; get deals on accommodations; and help each other with merch sales, travel logistics, and more.

What if you could set up a "residency" (or something similar) in another city for a couple of weeks to help pay bills while playing the areas around that city on off nights?

When most musicians think "tour," they think of being in a van for weeks on end and traveling from city to city. What if "tour" meant sleeping on a fellow musician's couch in NYC for a couple of weeks, playing several shows around New York and New Jersey, and then returning the favor and letting that musician stay at your house and play the area you're from?

Whether you play at a club 4,000 miles away from your home or are testing new material for those who pass by your local coffee shop as you play on the street outside, remember that your music needs to be heard. Don't let lack of money keep you from giving people the chance to hear it.

No Support or Encouragement

You will have some people in your life who think pursuing music is a really cool thing and believe in what you're doing. Others will see it as a hobby that won't lead to anything.

Some of your friends will be jealous of what you do. Others will judge harshly and think you're living in a fantasy world and are refusing to grow up or take responsibility for your life.

When it comes to encouragement, even if your friends and family are supportive of you, there are only so many times you can ask them to come to your gigs or help fund a new record.

So, when you're dealing with people and the energy they're throwing at you, on top of the stress that business-related tasks may cause, as well as your own self-doubt, how do you stay focused and keep moving forward?

The answer is to keep putting out music.

Why do this? The answer is twofold.

If you're constantly in the process of writing, recording, and performing music, you're focused more on those things than on other people's opinions of what you've done in the past.

Secondly, more music equals the potential for more fans. People take interest in those who are pursuing their dream—who are embarking on a journey. People are supportive of those who are moving forward.

Showing the world you're moving forward will attract both support and encouragement. If you do a gig and none of your friends or industry connections show up, but 100 strangers do, you're still touching lives. Those 100 people are spending money with you, getting involved with what you're doing, and providing you with forward momentum. This is support and encouragement.

Perfectionism

Perfectionism will destroy your creation faster than anything else can, because it strikes before what you do is even finished. Julia Cameron, author of *The Artist's Way* says, "Perfectionism is a refusal to let yourself move ahead. It is a loop—an obsessive, debilitating closed system that causes you to get stuck in the details of what you are writing or painting or making and to lose sight of the whole."

Here are three ways you can immediately begin dissolving the hold perfectionism may have over you:

Stop Comparing Yourself to Others – Like the Chi-Lites sing, "If everybody looked the same, we'd get tired of looking at each other." This applies to music too.

Do your thing. Don't worry about what other people are doing.

Nobody can do what you do. Another musician may be more technically proficient, but people don't buy music or come to shows based on that—they buy music and come to shows based on how these things make them feel.

Take Ownership – Own the fact that nothing is flawless and there will always be blemishes, no matter how many times you rewrite, re-record, or otherwise polish and prepare for release.

When you release something into the world, regardless of how good it is, you'll get feedback with opinions on how it can be improved. Take the feedback and, if it resonates with you, use it to make your next product better, but don't base your self-worth on it.

Take the Middle Ground – Don't take an "all or nothing" approach to what you do. Just because something isn't perfect doesn't mean it doesn't have worth.

Listen to the first AC/DC album *High Voltage*. It's one of the classic rock albums of all time and a lot of it is out of tune.

Ringo Starr, whom *Rolling Stone* readers picked as the fifth-best drummer of all time, described himself as "your basic offbeat drummer with funny fills."

War's classic song "Why Can't We Be Friends?" is off-key throughout, from the piano introduction to the vocals.

Focus on creating music that people connect with. That is far more valuable than technical perfection.

A song is always a work in progress. There will always be somebody better than you are. You will always find a need for something that costs more money than you currently have access to.

A song that is never released will never touch somebody. Nobody, regardless of how good, can do music in the way you can. The amount of money in your bank account is all you need to get going on some level.

Perfection is a process. Start where you are to get going with it.

Waiting for the Right Time

There is never the "perfect" time to do anything. If you are putting things on hold because you're waiting for enough money, waiting to write better songs, waiting until you're better at playing or performing, waiting until you have enough fans, or waiting until circumstances in your life change, think about this.

In every career, there are always external circumstances to deal with. If a fisherman in Alaska waited until there was perfect weather to take out his boat, he would never work. A surgeon's services aren't needed for a patient with perfect health. A gambler doesn't wait until after the dice are thrown to make a bet.

Feel the fear and move forward anyway. Trust that you have the needed skills to handle whatever comes up.

For example, let's say you've got some songs you want to record but not enough money for the studio you want. Are you going to let that stop you from moving forward? Record the songs in the best way your budget allows. If there is no budget, record them on your computer. Or get a job and do what it takes to get the money you need. Or charge the bill to a credit card.

It doesn't matter what you do, as long as you do *something*.

Fear of Rejection

The desire to be part of a group is part of our biology and goes back to a time when humans needed a tribal situation simply to survive. Today, thousands of years later, we still fear that not fitting into a certain mold (or getting certain reactions from others) means we will not be accepted.

Fear of being rejected manifests itself in different ways, such as comparing our skills to the skills of others. Many times, fear of rejection is paralyzing—rather than risk failure, we choose to do nothing.

But there is no "wrong" in the music. Just because a song doesn't connect with everybody doesn't mean it won't connect with somebody.

Not everybody is going to like you. The good news is that this is fine.

Careers in the music business are not built on keeping the majority of people happy; they are built on keeping some people very happy. This happens when you release music people feel is authentic and can deeply connect with.

Your music is an extension of you and your personality. If it's not being rejected by some people, you're not reaching enough people with it.

To overcome fear of rejection, focus on finding the community of people who will, most likely, really get and appreciate what you're doing. Cultivate relationships among the people within this group who enjoy your music. They are the people who matter and will help your marketing efforts by telling their friends about you.

Fear of Missing Out

It's amazing to think that you can make more money by catering to a small, targeted group of people than you can by trying to do something that is pleasing to everybody.

While this seems counterintuitive to many people, it is very real.

By isolating some people, it makes you more attractive to others. A great music business example of this is Insane Clown Posse. Police hate them, parents hate them, and the church hates them, but these things make them even more attractive to their fan base.

Does a teenager want to listen to the same music as his parents? No.

When you try to please everybody, you'll please nobody.

It can be scary to go "narrow and deep" with your music, especially if you've already had some success marketing to a general audience. However, within any general audience there are people who share common beliefs, traits, and opinions. If you can recognize these common characteristics and speak to them within your music, you'll create an even greater connection with your fans.

Fear of Making Wrong Decisions

Many musicians (maybe you are one of them) see "creative" and "business" as two different things. They put themselves into the creative category and leave the business side of things to others.

This mindset can be a hindrance when a musician needs to make a business-related decision.

When it comes to negotiating deals, ensuring you're not getting ripped off, and making good decisions on how to reinvest money into your career, you need to tap into a natural business sense you might have (but not know it) or cultivate a business sense. This will automatically happen when you treat your music like a business. The first step in this process is thinking about money—getting paid for gigs, making sure bills are paid on time, and having a dedicated bank account. Start with small things like these and work yourself up to the bigger business decisions.

Obviously, you can connect with people who are better at making business decisions than you are and let them handle these tasks for you. Do not let this keep you from learning the necessary skills to make business decisions for yourself. You don't have to know everything about the business end of music, but it's a good idea for you to have a general overview.

In the end, you'll never know if you're making a right decision (or a wrong one) until you make it. Still, you can develop the ability to feel a situation out ahead of time by practicing decision-making skills early and often in your music business career.

Even the best people make bad decisions. As you make more and more decisions regarding your career, you will also do this. Don't worry about making mistakes. The only thing you should worry about is whether or not you'll keep moving forward, regardless of the decision's outcome.

Limited Time and Energy

Even if you use every time-management system that exists, the reality is that you have a lot going on in your life and time in limited. Even with the best intentions, it can be difficult to do everything that needs to be done, especially if you're working a day job.

It gets frustrating when you have a dream, you know time is passing by, and it seems like music always gets pushed to the back because other things (especially the things that bring in more money than music) have to be a priority.

How do you fit it all in, or, at the very least, how do you stop being so frustrated or feeling hopeless when the progress is slow or only happens in small bursts?

Dealing with limited time and energy isn't just about prioritizing what makes you money—it's about prioritizing what makes you happy. This is often a balance of both music business and personal goals.

Being an international rock star requires a high degree of sacrifice that the majority of people simply aren't ready to commit to. With that said, there are options in the music business that may work just as well for you while allowing you to keep everything else in your life in order.

Get clear on what you really want. When you do this, the time and energy will work themselves out.

Lack of Trust

The act of pursuing a career in music will force you to take many leaps of faith. Countless times, you'll need to put your trust in other people. Most importantly, you'll need to trust yourself to make the big, bold decisions that will help move you forward in the direction you want to go.

When you do something like quit your job to pursue music, move from your small hometown to Nashville, or cash in your retirement savings to fund recording for a new album, you will likely have moments of self-doubt. During these times, rather than focusing on what could go wrong, give yourself credit for doing something so many people wouldn't have the courage to do. Focus on moving forward with your plans, and, at times like this, tap into your support system or create one made of people who can relate to what you're going through.

When you don't see growth (more sales, more people coming to the shows) for months, how do you trust in yourself and the process enough to keep going? This is a good time for you to look at interviews with musician role models and see how they successfully overcame low points in their careers.

If you want to grow your business, at some point, handing over non-music tasks to other people will become necessary. When you do so, you need to make common sense choices. This is your dream, and there is so much on the line to making it happen.

Passion for the music business, dedication to your career, and integrity are perhaps the most important qualities to look for when hiring somebody. Without these, all the experience in the world won't matter.

Anybody you work with should be honest and truly have your best interests at heart. It's fine to feel people out using your intuition, but always do your due diligence by getting references on people you're considering working with.

Music industry experience is important, but it can be acquired. A person can build a career off passion, dedication, and integrity.

When others join your business and begin to pursue their own agendas instead of yours, it can create the first crack in the foundation of trust. You can stop this from happening by knowing what you want, being confident about asking for it, and avoiding what others think is best for you (but doesn't feel right).

Strive to be clear with your communication and surround yourself with those who also communicate clearly. Straightforward, professional communication will help you grow trust with those you want to work with and help you avoid getting into situations with those who aren't on the same page as you.

Overwhelm

While music is an important part of the music business, things like marketing and developing a connection with fans are equally important. If you're in this business because you want to do music more than anything else and these things take you away from that, it can feel overwhelming.

How do you market yourself without feeling like all the tasks involved in doing so are taking over your life?

Perhaps you need to reframe what you think about music marketing. Think of it this way:

Music marketing is an extension of you and your music.

Seriously, it's as simple as that. It's a non-music extension of who you are and what you create. It's everything you and your music already are, but brighter, louder, faster, stronger, and taller.

Music marketing is Judas Priest wearing leather and riding around on motorcycles.

Music marketing is Diddy flying around in a private jet and drinking Courvoisier.

Music marketing is you *living* your music by doing whatever you do.

For a folk artist, it may be driving around in a van with a cooler of bulk food and a dog in the back. For a DJ, it may be related to your fashion or the neighborhood where you live.

Music marketing is coming up with a complete package that sells music, gets people to shows and makes money. That's it!

If you're feeling overwhelmed, simply understand that, although you may feel like you hate music marketing, you're already doing it—like it or not.

CONCLUSION

While technology has changed and the music industry has changed, there are a few things that will never change.

A strong relationship with fans will always be important.

People will always enjoy music, whether for listening, as a background for dancing, or as something to perform.

You will always need to have clarity on what you want in order to make it happen.

If you put your focus on the things that are consistent, timeless, and never change, you will be better able to navigate the things that do change.

FINAL THOUGHTS

The statement I'm about to make is going to sound obvious to most people, but it's something that I see artists often forget. If you can be one of the people who really gets it and takes these words to heart, you will have a much better career experience than the majority of musicians:

The music industry exists to help you succeed.

The "music industry" is not a mysterious entity that exists to frustrate you. It's a group of people, just like you, who love music. They are quick to see the appeal of what you're doing, willing to get in on the ground level, and will do the grunt work to help get others on board, if you are willing to work with them.

There are no bigger fans of music (and those who make it) than the people who work in the music industry.

A long career in the music industry requires co-creation with others. Even though your name may be listed as a writer, producer, or performer, it's important that you are aware of the contributions others are making toward your success in this business and acknowledge them.

Your audience is equally important.

Your fans are not random people who happened to be in the same place you're playing, and they don't purchase your music by accident. They show up because what you do makes them feel good.

Fans complete the cycle of the music business—you give by writing, recording, and performing, and they receive by listening, watching, and buying.

As an example, think about the very best show you've been to.

Perhaps it was something with just a singer/songwriter on stage in a small club, where everybody in the audience was silent and totally present with him or her during every note.

Or maybe it was something where an arena-sized audience was singing along with the act, such as Queen's "Live at Wembley" concert.

Freddie Mercury didn't need an arena filled with people to give a performance; he could have done it in your living room. But *somebody* would have had to be there with him, watching and listening, for it to be a truly great show.

No song, whether recorded in a studio or performed on stage, is complete without contribution, even if it's passive, from an audience. Whether people are sitting quietly or standing, jumping around, and yelling, without an audience, by definition, the performance doesn't exist.

If people aren't being affected by your music, you have nothing.

And when it comes to making money, remember:

There are opportunities to make money in the music business *everywhere*. You know this already. You've heard about them from fellow musicians and seen ads for them online and in musician magazines.

Film and television licensing, playing cruise ships, getting your song cut by a famous artist ... I could go on and on.

All of these opportunities have the *potential* to make money, and many musicians are making money in these very ways. You could make any (or all) of them happen for yourself, if you're willing to do the needed work.

But would doing so provide you with the career—and life—you want?

You've made it to the final pages of this book, which makes me think you want something more than chasing after a dollar sign. So let me tell you how to get it …

Focus.

Go after what you want with a laser-like focus.

You are in control of your career. Everything is in place for you to be successful in this business.

Get clear on what you want, and go after it.

If your dream is to license your music to film and television shows, do it.

If your dream is to have a dedicated following that buys everything you release, create it.

If your dream is to get your songs cut by another artist, go for it.

Just don't say "yes" to something simply because there is the potential to make a few bucks—there is potential in everything.

Say "yes" when opportunity comes your way because it helps you realize your dream and affords you the life you want. Never compromise. The money will be there.

IT'S YOUR JOB TO KEEP IN TOUCH WITH FANS
(NOT THE OTHER WAY AROUND)

Included in this section is information about how to keep connected with your most valuable asset—your fans.

In this section, I give you very specific advice, including sample scripts and promotions you can use, to reach out to your fans via email, postal mail, and phone and in person with the purpose of getting them to buy music, attend live performances, and otherwise spend money with you.

HOW TO USE E-MAIL EFFECTIVELY

Email is a great way to communicate, because it's easy, fast, and almost free. If you have a last-minute gig, you can get the word out quickly. If you send out a message today, you can have a packed house tonight—if you reach the right people.

The problem most musicians have when using email is they're not reaching the right people. "Everybody" is not the right people.

Would you send a postcard to somebody in Nashville to let them know about your upcoming gig in Los Angeles? No.

So why do so many musicians do this via email?

For the same reasons people love email so much. It's easy, fast, and almost free.

There's an old saying that "free advice often is the most expensive." The same goes for marketing.

You can send 10,000 emails just as easily as you can send 10. Just because you can do something doesn't mean it's a good idea, though, and sending emails definitely applies here.

If you're not getting the response you want from your email marketing, make sure you're sending the right message to the right people.

What does this mean? It means you need to segment your mailing list.

SEGMENT YOUR MAILING LIST

You should have a different mailing list for every city you play. This will allow you to not only send out targeted messages regarding your upcoming gigs, but it will also let you build more rapport with your fans by getting personal.

The following is an example of a personalized email you should send out about three days before your show:

SUBJECT: See you Friday, <<NAME>>?

Hey, <<NAME>> -

<<YOUR NAME>> from <<BAND NAME>> here. Quick message for you ...

We're back in Memphis on this Friday (the 13th) and playing BB King's on Beale. Show starts at 10:30 p.m., but doors open at 8 p.m., so show up early if you want, because we'll be hanging out *at the bar, meeting people, and signing copies of our new album, <<ALBUM NAME>>.*

It's been a couple of months since we've been through Memphis. Last time we were in town, we dropped by this great BBQ place called Rendezvous, so we can't wait to get back.

Heard from some folks that Rendezvous isn't actually the best BBQ in town. Hit me back and let me know if you agree, because we're only there a couple of days and we want the best!

See you Friday!

<<YOUR NAME>>

PS - We played Chunky, Mississippi, a couple of nights ago. One of our fans there dared us to play "Toxic" by Britney Spears, so we did. <<LINK>> to check it out.

PPS - If you have a cover song (or one of our songs) you want us to play in Memphis, let me know, OK?

NOTE: Feel free to fill in your details and send out a copy of this message to your fans. In fact, use all the examples I give in this chapter. Be aware that a lot of the people reading this book are going to do the same, so you'll be better off figuring out why this message works and creating your own version of it.

WHY THIS MESSAGE WORKS

Here's a breakdown of this message's five different elements. You don't have to have all of them to ensure a successful mailing, but the more you have, the greater your chance of success.

1. **Like music, timing of any kind of message you send to your fans is important.**

   This particular message is something that I'd send out three or four days before the show, especially if the show is on a weekend. You want it to "land" on a Tuesday or Wednesday, which is a low-volume day for email and will help your message stand out from the dozens, hundreds, or even thousands of other messages your fans will receive that week. Beyond that, the timing will give people enough opportunity to plan to come see you, but not so much that they'll forget those plans.

2. The Name Drop

Your goal with any communication is to further a relationship. The person on the other end of this email isn't a nameless, faceless entity designed to fill space at one of your shows; it's a human with real feelings and emotion.

Referring to somebody by his/her name gets attention. Emails with a name in the subject get opened more than any other type of email. And emails with a name at the top of the message area get read more often than any type of email.

Take advantage of this.

3. The Subject

This subject works for a couple of reasons. First, as mentioned above, because it includes the recipient's name. Beyond that, though, it sets the stage for the entire purpose of the message, which is to see this person at a gig on Friday. All the information within the message body is backed up by this subject, which makes your communication very powerful.

4. One Person

Write emails to your list in the same way you'd write an email to a friend. Direct your message to a single person, not everybody.

DO THIS: "We'd love to see you on Friday."

DON'T DO THIS: "We'd love to see all our fans on Friday."

5. One Message

The example above has a single purpose – get people to the Memphis show on Friday the 13th. That's it.

Don't confuse people by telling them about other shows or the albums you have for sale or by asking them to "like" your Facebook page. Give them the message, then back that message up.

Here is an example of an email to send as a follow-up to the email above, which will not only get more people to your shows, but also allow you to connect with them on a level that most acts never do.

Send this the day after you send the previous email (2-3 days before the show):

SUBJECT: Your first drink is on me, <<NAME>>.

Hey, <<NAME>> -

<<YOUR NAME>> from <<BAND NAME>> again. I forgot to tell you something yesterday ...

As I mentioned, we'll be back in Memphis this Friday (the 13th), playing BB King's on Beale. Show starting at 10:30 p.m., and hanging out at the bar, meeting people, and signing copies of our new album, <<ALBUM NAME>> starting at 8 p.m.

What I forgot to tell you is that, if you get there by 9 p.m., YOUR FIRST DRINK IS ON ME!

No catch. When you pay the door guy, he'll give you a ticket you can redeem at the bar for anything you want—your favorite mixed drink, a really snobby European import, a shot of Jägermeister ... Anything!

See you Friday!

<<YOUR NAME>>

PS - This is for you and any of your friends, too. So feel free to bring along as many people as you'll want. We'll take care of all of them, just like we'll take care of you! :)

This is just one of many ways for you to take the relationship you have with fans from a one-way, they-watch-what-you're-doing situation to something that is more interactive.

DO E-MAIL MARKETING THE RIGHT WAY

If you're on another music act's mailing list, chances are you've got plenty examples of what you shouldn't be doing in your inbox. I'm on dozens of lists, whether I signed up for them or not, and it blows my mind to see people doing the same stupid things, over and over again.

Here are a few email marketing rules ...

1. **If somebody didn't sign up for your mailing list, don't put him or her on it.**

   Don't assume that, at worst, people won't mind you adding their names to a list. And don't assume that, at best, they'll appreciate the gesture. People are busy. If they want to get information from you, they'll let you know.

   When it comes to building your mailing list, it's very easy to fall into the trap of thinking that 100 people is better than 10 and 10 people is better than a couple. In this case, quality trumps quantity. It's far better to have 10 people who care and are actually waiting to hear from you than 10,000 people who have no clue who you are.

   You won't win people over with a bulk email, so don't bother.

   This is important, so I'm going to repeat it ...

   If somebody didn't sign up for your mailing list, don't put that person on it.

It doesn't matter if a club owner (or anybody else) says something like, "keep in touch." "Keep in touch" means they want to have a two-way relationship, not get a one-sided email blast.

2. If somebody lives more than 50 miles away from the gig you're promoting, assume they don't care.

The people receiving your emails are busy individuals with things to do. They don't care about every place you're playing this month; they care only about the places that are close to them.

3. If you're playing a weekly gig, you don't need to let people know every week.

You play every week at the same place. We get it. The reason nobody is showing up isn't because you're not sending email; the problem is you're not making that gig special, turning it into an "event" that people want to be part of.

4. You MUST have a one-click unsubscribe option.

Don't make people work to get off your mailing list. If they're not interested in what you have to offer, you want them off your list so you can focus on people who want to hear from you. In addition, you'll lose signups from people who are "on the fence" about what you have, because nobody wants to sign up for something they'll never be able to get off of.

5. You MUST use a reliable, third-party mailing list service.

As you know, junk email is a big problem. Because of this, it is more difficult than ever to successfully send commercial email messages.

If you want the majority of your emails to land in inboxes instead of being blocked by spam filters, you need to send them though a reliable, third-party mailing list service that specializes in getting emails delivered. In addition to the benefit of getting your messages into the hands of the people who want them, these companies will also provide services to keep you from violating email marketing laws, such as "double-opt-in" verification of all new signups and one-click unsubscribe options.

Beyond keeping you legal, a third-party mailing list service will also be able to provide you with marketing tools, such as the ability to track how many of your messages get opened and how many people click on the links inside your messages. You'll get powerful "mail merge" options so you can send "personal" messages, using the recipient's name, city, or other information you have collected, within any messages you send.

There are several options for third-party mailing list services available, and I have recommended providers listed in my resource guide for musicians at MusicMarketing.com.

Once you have selected a mailing list host, create a signup form to let people join your mailing list via your website. This is something that can usually be done via the dashboard within your mailing list account. When creating your mailing list signup form, you'll want to, at a minimum, ask for "First Name" and "Email." If you're playing in multiple markets, it's a good idea to also get a ZIP code from everybody, so you'll be able to segment the list based on where your recipients are located.

GIVE PEOPLE A REASON TO SIGN UP FOR YOUR LIST

People today are bombarded with email. Because of this, it is getting more and more difficult to get people to sign up for an online mailing list. To help convince people it's a good opportunity, you may want to offer free music, free tickets to a show, or another bonus for signing up.

A great product to give people is a documentary-style video that includes live performances. It not only entertains people who watch it, but the "documentary" parts of the video sell viewers on you and your music by letting them get to know who you are. With that improved connection with you, everything else you do is that much more interesting to them.

Note that, for maximum results, what you give away has to be something people would pay for. In fact, it will help your credibility (and signup rates) if there is a "money option" for what you're giving away for free. That way people can verify the monetary value personally.

For the documentary idea (or any video product), the "money option" is to have a DVD for sale on Amazon or another online retailer. When you do this, you're proving to fans, "Everybody else is paying $X for this, but you're getting it free."

This is easier than it may sound. You can use a print-on-demand service, like Kunaki or CreateSpace, which handles all fulfillment and eliminates a big upfront cost and stocking issues.

You can see an example of this at MusicMarketing.com, where I give away a free audio book on music marketing to people who sign up for my list. Or you can go to Amazon and get the same audio book on CD for $10.49.

FINAL THOUGHTS ON SENDING E-MAILS TO YOUR FANS

When sending ANY marketing email, you need to have a purpose. (Getting the recipient to come to a specific show, for example.) I call this the "TOT Method." TOT stands for "the one thing."

In other words, when sending an email, DO NOT bombard the recipient with a ton of choices. Don't send a long-ass email talking about your upcoming gig this weekend, another gig next month, the new album for sale, and a new T-shirt design. Give them a single option to think about.

"Do you want to come to the show this weekend?"

"Do you want to buy a T-shirt?"

"Do you want to buy the new album?"

One email = one choice ... ALWAYS!

SENDING POSTCARDS

Sophie Tucker (1886–1966) was a Russian/Ukrainian-born American singer and actress. Known for her stentorian delivery of comical and risqué songs, she was one of the most popular entertainers in America during the first two-thirds of the 20th century. She was widely known by the nickname "The Last of the Red Hot Mamas." Her song, "My Yiddishe Mama," was banned by Hitler— ... which made it even more popular.

Tucker's early career consisted of playing piano and singing burlesque and vaudeville tunes, at first in blackface. She later said that this was at the insistence of theater managers, who said she was "too fat and ugly" to be accepted by an audience in any other context. She sang songs that acknowledged her size, such as "Nobody Loves a Fat Girl, but Oh How a Fat Girl Can Love."

That's what people think of when they think of Sophie Tucker ... But what most people don't know is what a great marketer she was.

As Sophie toured the United States, she would take down the names and addresses of the people in her audience. Before she would come to town again, she would send people personal postcards letting them know when and where she would be performing.

She was a big fan of handwritten letters and postcards, sending them to keep in touch with not only fans but business associates as well.

It's a good method to let people know what you're up to, and it still works today. In fact, it works better than ever today, since much of our "postcard" communication has been replaced by emails, text messages, and phone calls, and it's easier for your message to stand out.

Email is easy to delete ... and that assumes it gets opened in the first place. Text messages all look the same. And who is going to call every single fan to come to a show?

Postcards allow you to get your message out quickly, easily, and cheaply. A postcard is something that can sit on a table for days (or even weeks), reminding somebody to come to your show. And it's not as easy to throw away as hitting the delete button on an email.

Does it cost more money than an email? Yes. But it's not how much something costs that matters—it's how much it makes you. And postcards make musicians money.

Getting started with postcards ...

The first thing you're going to need is addresses to send to. These shouldn't be just any addresses, either. You're not sending out postcards just for fun; you're sending out postcards to make something specific happen, such as getting people to a certain show or having them download your new album.

To get addresses, I suggest you start with your best customers, the people who are already coming to see you live.

At your next show, when the crowd is at its peak, try this script:

"Are you having as much fun as we are?" (Wait for them to say yes.)

"We should get together soon and do it again. You think so?" (Wait for them to say yes.)

"Next time, how about if you let us buy your first drink?" (Wait for them to say yes.)

"We're playing here again at (CLUB NAME) in (NUMBER OF WEEKS) on (DATE OF NEXT SHOW). At the back of the room, at our merch table, there is a clipboard. Fill out your name and address, and I'll send you an invite along with a free drink ticket."

You don't have to follow the exact script, but I do want you to understand the psychology behind it, so if you change it up you can get similar results.

The request for addresses starts with a sales trick known as a "yes ladder." This asks the crowd questions to which the only answer is "yes" and warms them up for an additional "yes" when you make your offer.

Beyond that, you're planting the seeds for a successful follow-up show by giving a specific date as well as a countdown to it, so fans will know exactly when you'll be back. This is optional, but for best results, play the same club, since everybody in your audience will know where it is, is comfortable there, and will easily be able to make it back.

As far as actually sending the postcards, if you've got 200 or less, this is an easy print job for a copy shop like FedEx Office. Make a postcard using any word processor software, then have them print four to a sheet on color "cardboard" paper and cut them.

For best results, hand-address the postcard and use a "live" stamp. (This is a traditional stamp with a color image, like a flag or a bird or a flower—not something from a postal meter or barcode postage, like Stamps.com.) Put a personal note like "Thanks for your support, (NAME)!" on the other side.

If you've got thousands of addresses, it may be time to move everything to a mailing house. See USPS.com or search "direct mail" for more information.

In my opinion, this is the absolute best way to connect with fans. It's inexpensive, easy, and scalable—and almost nobody is doing it, so it will be easy for you to stand out from other acts trying to get attention with more "modern" methods like email.

PHONE CALLS

Thanks to mobile phones and voice mail, it's easier than ever to reach out to fans via a phone call.

There was a time when getting a phone call was a big deal. And getting a long-distance phone call was a very big deal.

Today, we're more connected than ever before, but, like postal mail, much of the communication that was once done via phone is now done via other media, such as email or text messages. The "phone" part of a mobile phone, for many people, is an afterthought.

So why bother?

Because, afterthought or not, almost everybody has a phone and very few people are getting calls from their favorite artists. When you do use a phone in this way, it stands out. Your message will have a better chance of connecting because you'll cut through the noise of text messages and emails.

When you're building your mailing list, don't be afraid to ask for a phone number in addition to a postal address. If a person doesn't want to give it to you, he doesn't have to. But if people do, it's a great way to build a relationship.

We live in a busy world, and most calls you make will go to voice mail. Because of this, it's fairly easy to reach a lot of people in a short amount of time.

Here is a phone message for somebody who has just seen your show and signed up for your mailing list:

> *"Hey, (NAME). This is (YOUR NAME) from (BAND NAME). Thanks for coming to (CLUB NAME) last night. Hope you had a good time. We're back there in (NUMBER OF WEEKS) on (DATE OF NEXT SHOW). Your first drink is on us, so watch for*

a ticket for that in your mailbox around (ONE WEEK BEFORE DATE OF NEXT SHOW). See you then!"

Again, like any of the scripts I'm including here, you don't have to follow this one verbatim. Once again, I do want you to understand the psychology behind it, though, so you can change it up and still get good results.

First, you're using the person's name. This automatically gets people tuned in and more receptive to hear what you have to say.

Next, you're reminding them how you connected and what a great time it was. Then you're letting them know when and where it will happen again, planting a seed that will help make your next reminder stick more easily.

You're setting yourself up for reciprocity (in the form of coming to your next show) with a free drink and giving them specific instructions on how you'll be contacting them next.

Getting started with phone calls ...

Yes, making calls will take some time. You're building personal connections with your fans that can last a lifetime, though, so when you consider what you'll be getting in return, it's time well spent.

How to do it:

1. Purchase a regular mobile phone or a prepaid phone exclusively for calling fans.

2. Because most phones today have Caller ID and you'll likely get callbacks, record a voice mail encouraging people to go to your website for a free download.

3. If you want to cut down on the number of messages people leave for you, let them know Twitter is the best and quickest way to get in touch with you. This will help you manage

expectations, since it's doubtful you'll be able to call everybody back and it's much easier to handle a large volume of people when messages are limited to 140 characters.

4. Start dialing.

What happens when things take off and you have more people than you can personally call? Google "voice broadcast" for options. Although these "robo calls" have a bad reputation in the media, I have successfully used them for many large campaigns and gotten good results that were pleasing to all parties involved, including the message recipients.

With that said, a voice broadcast can burn through a list of thousands within minutes. If you don't do it right, you'll agitate a lot of people. Use good judgement!

AUDIO MESSAGES

The primary method most musicians use to communicate with fans is text. This includes printed interviews, flyers, and emails. You can add new life to these messages by including an audio component.

The easiest way to start communicating with your fans via audio is via a phone "hotline." This is an old school method of connecting with fans, but because almost nobody is doing it today, it has a novelty element that gets results.

A phone hotline is a prerecorded message that people get when they call a phone number. If you have a dedicated phone line attached to a traditional answering machine or voice mail, you can easily set one up.

A phone hotline has several uses ...

Outgoing Messages:

- **Upcoming Shows** – This is the most common use for a phone hotline. At one time, it was great for getting the word out quickly about new tour dates. However, with the advent of the Internet, it is not nearly as effective to use in this way as it once was.

The only time I recommend using a phone hotline for upcoming shows is when you're an established act, you're about to announce a tour, and there is a lot of anticipation regarding where you'll be playing. In a case like this, make the announcement available at a scheduled time and move on to using your phone hotline for something else.

- **New Music Preview** – One of the great things about the Internet is that it has allowed musicians to let fans preview high-quality samples of music. While this has its advantages, there are also advantages to sharing only lower-quality music samples.

  The best example I can give to illustrate this point is a movie that leaves something to the imagination, such as *Jaws*. If you're not familiar with the story of *Jaws*, it's about a fictional summer resort town and a giant, man-eating great white shark that terrorizes the people on vacation there. The most frightening scenes in Jaws never show you the shark. The film relies instead on the imagination of viewers, which is far more developed and scary than anything a movie studio could come up with, to get a reaction. Similarly, letting your fans preview music in a raw format, such as over the telephone, will force them to use their imaginations about how great your music will sound when experienced in a higher-fidelity format. It's a little taste that will leave people wanting more.

- **Tour Updates** – This is a different take on what you should be doing with Twitter or your blog. Simply post check-ins throughout the tour to let people know of your progress and get out important messages. For the right act, this can be done multiple times per day.

  For a true fan, this can be huge. Imagine, for example, a rabid Taylor Swift fan waiting for the show that night in her hometown. She has the album, she has the T-shirts, and she's been waiting all year to see Taylor live in concert. In the middle of the show, from the stage, Taylor calls the phone hotline to check in and leave a message to let all the people who couldn't be there know how it's going. She takes photos, posts them via Twitter, and encourages people to go view them. Or she gives people a special link where they can get exclusive material. While your situation may not be exactly like this, you can still use something similar to build connection with your fans and keep them engaged.

- **Philosophical Messages** – This one works best with bands that subscribe to a specific religious philosophy. For example, if you're in the Christian genre, something like a "Daily Devotional" or "Bible Verse of the Day" is great.

  Other acts that can really benefit from this include those with a strong social or political philosophy. If you're somebody who would work well on FOX News (John Rich, Hank Williams Jr., or Ted Nugent, for example), this is perfect for you. Alternatively, it works equally well for comedy or children's artists. Who doesn't love a "Joke of the Day" line?

Incoming Messages:

- **Fan Questions** – Your fans have questions for you, and this is the perfect way to get them.

  How it works: People call in and record a question, and you answer it via a recorded message on the phone hotline or, if you want to get people using multiple types of communication (which will build rapport between you and them), your website.

- **Fan Answers** – This is one of my favorite ways to use a phone hotline. Instead of having fans ask you something, get them to tell you something.

Levi's did a huge promotion in the '90s using this technique to market its "Levi's 501, shrink-to-fit" jeans. They set up a toll-free hotline and asked people to answer the question, "What do you do in your Levi's 501 jeans?"

There was just one problem ... Over 50 percent of the calls were "inappropriate."

But is that really a problem? Maybe not for you. Even if you can't use the messages people leave, you can still get good publicity out of something like this by giving the media a good story to talk about. At worst, this is what you'll end up with. At best, you'll get fans engaged and get some great information about what your fans really want.

Suggested questions:

"What do you do while listening to our music?"

"Which song should we release as our next single?"

"Which cover song should we record?"

"Which song should we make a music video for?"

Why a phone hotline? That's the question you may be asking yourself. After all, with so much new technology available, what's the point of using something so dated? This is something "local bands" (before the word "independent" was used to describe non-signed acts) used back in the 1980s. Why go back in time?

These are good questions. Here are five reasons you should think about adding a phone hotline to your promotion plan:

- **The "Extra Step" Principle** – Remember what your mother used to say ... "Nothing good comes easy."

  The phone hotline is basic psychology at work. People who have worked to achieve something enjoy it more. The more steps you can lead people through in order to consume your message, the more they'll enjoy it.

In addition, people who have worked for something are more loyal to it. When you've invested your time and money into something, you're less likely to go somewhere else.

- **Easy Access to Phones** – As popular as the Internet is, the majority of people can still access a phone more often and more easily.

- **It's Memorable** – A phone hotline is something different from what the typical musician is currently doing to promote his music (e.g., website, Facebook, Twitter, etc.). Also, the fact that your message is coming through a non-computer source makes it even more memorable.

- **It's Exclusive** – The "Internet" goes out to everybody. A phone message has the appearance of going to a single person or, at the very most, a few people. This "exclusivity" feels good to fans.

- **High Conversion Rate** – The more ways you can get people to consume your message, the more likely it is that your message will be received and acted on. The phone hotline, along with online videos, emails, postcards, blog entries, and live shows, is an important aspect of a complete promotion.

Getting started with audio messages ...

While there are several options for creating a phone hotline, the fastest and easiest (you can set one up in about 10 minutes) is through a service like Skype or Google Voice. Either will give you a number and allow you to record an outgoing message, just like an answering machine or traditional voice mail.

The easiest way to get people to start using your phone hotline is to have previews of songs you are working on. This will let fans be part of the "creation" process of writing and recording as well as get them invested in the music you're preparing to release.

If you're in a religious band, or social or political issues are a big part of your act, I suggest starting with a hotline you update daily with devotionals or other issue-oriented messages of interest to your audience.

Once you've chosen what type of messages you want to broadcast, simply give out your hotline number on any postcards, emails, flyers, or other communication you send. In additional, print it in your liner notes and any advertising you do.

Beyond the phone hotline, start using audio messages within emails, web pages, and blog posts you create. Doing this will give your fans an additional way to consume your message, which will make it stick better.

Visit MusicMarketing.com and check out my resource section for a list of recommended audio message tools.

TEXT MESSAGES

Because the majority of people today own a mobile phone and many users take them everywhere they go, texting is a great way to reach people. Text messaging is instant and to the point.

A text message is perfect for a last-minute push to local people about a gig that starts in just a few hours. Sending a message like, "*<<YOUR NAME>> from <<BAND NAME>> here. Hope to see you at <<CLUB NAME>> tonight at 8 p.m.*" can be very effective.

And if you want something even more effective ...

> "*<<YOUR NAME>> from <<BAND NAME>> here. Hope to see you at <<CLUB NAME>> tonight at 8 p.m. Show this text for free admission.*"

> "*<<YOUR NAME>> from <<BAND NAME>> here. Hope to see you at <<CLUB NAME>> tonight at 8 p.m. Show this text at door for a free drink.*"

Getting started with text messages ...

There are plenty of companies that offer services to let you market via text message. If you're just testing the waters though, Twitter can be used as a poor man's version of this. It's not quite as effective as using a company that specializes in text message marketing, but it's free and a good way to see if this method of promotion is for you. Since many people check their Twitter feeds on their mobile phones, you can reach them any time.

How to do it: Set up an account on Twitter for each city that you play. For example, if your band is called Band XYZ, and you play Nashville, Memphis, and Atlanta, set up three accounts:

1. BandXYZ-Nashville

2. BandXYZ-Memphis

3. BandXYZ-Atlanta

Tell your fans to follow the Twitter account that corresponds with the city they live in (or are closest to) to get exclusive updates on upcoming shows.

Just booked a show in Nashville? Let "BandXYZ-Nashville" know about it.

Playing tonight in Memphis? Send "BandXYZ-Memphis" a reminder a few hours before the show.

Did you record the show you did in Atlanta last night? Let "BandXYZ-Atlanta" know they can download it on your website. Have some photos of the show posted? Let them know that too.

As you can see, it's easy to reach out to people, multiple times, with content that is relevant to them. As people who follow you can see other people on the follow list, Twitter is also a great place for fans to connect with other fans.

VIDEO MESSAGES

We live in a visual society. The television is the most influential appliance in American homes.

The "typical" person reads about four books per year, with 25 percent of people having read no books in the last year. According to Nielsen, in 2009, the average American spent 153 hours per month watching television. And YouTube is the third most popular site on the Internet.

In short, if you want to take advantage of this situation, you need to be making video messages.

One of the great things about a site like YouTube is that people are OK with "poor-quality" videos. In fact, poor video quality can actually be a benefit, believe it or not, because people associate it with being more authentic than the slick, well-produced content from major studios.

Sure, it's great if you're skilled with a video camera, but it's not necessary to be Steven Spielberg in order to have success, so don't let that lack of skill stop you. People go to a site like YouTube for content that can't be found anywhere else, and that's exactly what you can provide.

Options for video content:

- **In the Studio** – If you're in a recording studio, you should have the video camera running. It doesn't matter if it's a pro studio or something you've set up with a home computer; you have an opportunity to get people excited about what you're recording by showing them the process.

- **Soundchecks** – This is something most fans have heard of and are curious about but have never experienced. Let them.

- **Behind the Music** – Every song has a story. Every album has a story. Tell the story.

- **Unplugged** – Whether you're lounging in the living room, fooling around on acoustic guitars, or doing a more "professional" performance, people want to see it.

- **Rehearsals** – Another aspect of the business that fans know exists but few actually see. You're doing it anyway, so you might as well videotape it. Use what you get to give fans a different perspective on you and get them more attached to what you're doing.

- **Live Shows** – You should record a video of every performance you have, if for no other reason than to review it, pick every aspect of it apart, and improve on your weak spots. And if you get something pretty good, share it.

- **Backstage** – Whether you're surrounded by groupies or an overbearing stage mom, this is an aspect of the show that fans love to see.

- **On Tour** – As you know, there is a lot more to a tour than playing songs on stage. While this may seem boring to you, your fans are interested. Ideas for this kind of video include filming yourself at truck stops, tourist attractions, cheap hotels, expensive hotels, and restaurants. If you get pulled over by the cops, have a camera running.

Let people experience what you're living, and bring them into your story. We're talking short, 3-to-5-minute videos here, not a feature-length documentary film. Every aspect of it doesn't have to be that exciting; it's interesting because people want to know what life on tour is like. The goal is to connect with people on a deeper level and show them what you go through to play a show, not give them a false picture of a 24/7 party.

- **Cribs** – You've seen the show on MTV. Show your fans something more authentic. If you're uncomfortable with giving people a tour of your entire house, try just your bedroom, kitchen, or home studio.

- **Fan Q&A** – Fans have questions. You have answers. Videotape them.

- **News Hijack** – This works best for acts with a social or religious message, but it will work for anybody with an opinion. If you have a song about a certain issue that is in the news or an opinion about something that everybody is talking about, make a video and jump into the discussion.

  This works very well for acts with a strong political philosophy. If you're somebody who would work well on FOX News (John Rich, Hank Williams Jr., or Ted Nugent, for example), this is perfect for you. Alternatively, if you're on the other side of the political spectrum, there are a lot of people who will be very glad to hear from you also.

- **Philosophical Messages** – This one works well with acts that subscribe to a specific religious philosophy. For example, if you're in the Christian genre, something like a "Daily Devotional" or "Bible Verse of the Day" is great.

  Acts in "long-tail" genres that subscribe to nonreligious belief systems can also benefit from these types of videos. For example, acts in the genre I refer to as "Sober Music." If "recovery" is part of your identity, you can help a lot of people and connect with them by making videos talking about this message.

- **Music Lessons** – Musicians can get so close to what they're doing on a daily basis that it can be easy to forget what it was like not to be able to make music. "How to play music" is one of the most popular topics online, so a video teaching people how to make that happen can help you expand your audience in a big way. Videos can be everything from general tips to very specific lessons that teach people how to play your songs.

- **Cover Songs** – YouTube is the number-one music search engine online. Take advantage of it by posting covers of popular songs.

- **Cook Something** – Again, the entire purpose of posting videos is to connect with people. There is (almost) nothing more intimate than sharing a meal with somebody. And since you can't share food via a video, show people how to cook some.

Getting started with video messages ...

As mentioned above, the popularity of YouTube has helped lower the standards of what people expect from video. It's perfectly acceptable to shoot something with an iPhone, so assuming you have an iPhone or other mobile device that has the ability to record video, start there. It doesn't have to be perfect.

With that said, if you can create something of quality, by all means do so. Don't get so caught up in perfecting every element of it that it never sees the light of day, though. People want to connect with other people way more than they want a slick video. A few "mistakes" in what you release will actually help you to do that. People will find it to be more authentic.

The biggest issues most online videos have are light, sound, and editing.

The solutions:

Purchasing an inexpensive "soft box" kit will take care of basic lighting issues.

You need a mic better than the one inside your camera. As a musician, I'm sure you can figure out an option that will work well.

Basic software, such as Apple's iMovie, can handle any editing for the types of videos I am suggesting.

If you want to go further with videos, bring in a professional. You're a musician, not a videographer. Stick to what you do best.

MAKE FANS FEEL IMPORTANT

The relationships you have with fans are more important than anything else you're doing in the music business, including the music itself. Without fans, you have no career.

If you take care of people, they'll take care of you. Here is how you can build quality relationships with fans and make them feel important:

- **Reply to Messages** – Fans of your music know you're busy, so they don't always expect you to reply to fan mail or other messages they send. Because of this, a reply is extra powerful when it comes to showing them how much they are valued.

- **Be an Active Participant in Social Media** – Don't just have your people send out a generic message about when you'll be performing, where fans can purchase a new album, or links to great press. Instead, get involved on a more personal level by participating in discussions, "liking" Facebook posts you relate to, and thanking people when they post photos from your shows or mention you in posts.

- **Birthday Cards** – Handwritten cards are an over-the-top way to show that somebody is valued and will give you days, weeks, or even months of benefit, as people often save them. If you're not yet asking for date of birth when you have people sign up for your mailing list, you can start by posting "happy birthday" messages on fans' Facebook walls.

- **Thank You Card** – If you're selling music and other merchandise directly, let people know their purchases are appreciated by writing, "Thank you, <<NAME>>!" on the outside of the package as well as including a handwritten card letting them know you appreciate the support!

- **Bonus with Purchase** – If you're selling music and other merchandise directly, include a bonus with every purchase. A small gift, such as a "sampler album" or a voucher that can be exchanged for show tickets won't cost much and will provide a high return on investment, since it will help you to sell more in the future and will build your relationship with fans in a big way.

- **Charity** – In May 2010, a massive flood hit Nashville, causing about $1.6 billion in damage and displacing thousands of people. Shortly thereafter, there were benefit concerts by acts like Garth Brooks, Taylor Swift, and Carrie Underwood. Doing this not only raised a lot of money to help relief efforts but also showed these artists valued the people in the city that had helped put them on the map.

  There are opportunities like this happening all the time. Show people that you'll help take care of them in a time of need, and they'll take care of you.

- **Follow-up Coupon** – The best time to sell somebody something is right after they've purchased something similar. If you're selling music and other merchandise directly, send a "follow-up coupon" shortly thereafter for a discount on other merchandise. You'll increase your sales (and income) as well as show appreciation for the people supporting you by giving them better pricing than everybody else.

- **Adjust Approach Based on Feedback** – Fans, like all people, want to be heard. If they make suggestions, listen.

- **Be Available** – After your shows, stick around to sign albums and other merchandise, take photos, and show your appreciation to the people who came to see you.

- **Exclusive Releases/Products** – Everybody wants to feel special. Create exclusive music releases and products for people who join your mailing list or purchase music and other merchandise from you.

- **Loyalty Rewards** – Recognize your best customers by giving away free tickets to shows, creating exclusive music releases, and performing exclusive sets, such as "meet and greet" acoustic performances or members-only sound checks before shows.

Never neglect the partnership between you and your fans. Take care of them, and you will always have a career in the music business.

MUSIC DOESN'T SELL ITSELF

HOW TO MAKE MONEY SELLING YOUR MUSIC AND MERCH

As you've probably already found out, while it may appear to do so at times, music doesn't sell itself. Just because you've recorded a few great songs and put together an album doesn't guarantee people will care enough to spend money on it.

This chapter is about making people care enough so they do.

THE LIVE SHOW EXPERIENCE

Even with advances in music distribution and video, performing live is still the best way to sell recorded music. A live performance allows you to reach dozens, hundreds, and even thousands of people at once. It's an extremely effective "one-to-many" marketing solution. In addition, because people in the audience are paying for the experience of watching you, it's also one of the most cost-effective advertising strategies available to musicians.

If you're not playing live, you're leaving money on the table. Beyond that, you're missing out on a valuable opportunity to connect with fans in a way that your website, emails, interviews, photos, recorded music, and any other type of merchandising you have can't do.

The more ways you can communicate with your audience, the better rapport and connection you'll have with them. An audio recording of your music is great, but it can only be heard. A photo of your band is great, but it can only be seen. A live show connects you to an audience by engaging all senses.

A person in the audience will see you—and everything else around him or her. If you have people in the audience whom he finds visually attractive, this will add to his enjoyment of your show. If she likes the way the venue looks, she'll associate that good feeling with your music. Your fan will smell the fog machine on stage, stale beer on the floor, and cigarette smoke in the air. He'll smell sweat from the guy to his left, perfume on the woman to his right, the deep fryer in the kitchen, and food on the table. It's all of this, plus the music she heard, that make up the experience taken home after your show.

THE IMPORTANCE OF SOCIAL PROOF

When you see somebody walking down the street with headphones on, you have no idea what he is listening to. When somebody is at a live show, that person is surrounded by people listening to the same thing, and this "social proof" helps that music be better received, since it lets people know it's OK to enjoy it. In addition, being in a group situation forms a camaraderie and class consciousness among people.

A live show is something people rarely attend alone. It's the perfect opportunity for fans to tell others about your music and bring their friends along to experience it for themselves. And should that happen, you'll piggyback on the goodwill and already-established relationships among these people. If somebody experiences your live show with people they already like, they'll transfer those good feelings toward your music.

Finally, a live show is something that cannot be pirated. The only way to really experience it is to show up personally. Because of this, don't worry about people recording your performance or taking photographs. Instead, encourage them to do this, as it will be a catalyst for word-of-mouth promotion and grow your audience exponentially.

BEST EXAMPLES OF SELLING MUSIC AND MERCH AT LIVE SHOWS

People who have a good time at your live show will want to continue the experience, even after the show is over. They can do this by purchasing recorded music or other merchandise.

Once you get good at selling merchandise at a live show, you'll be able to turn a profit on "loser gigs" that, if you were making money only at the door or via a guarantee, wouldn't be cost effective. This will greatly increase your competitive advantage and enable you to play shows and reach fans you wouldn't have been able to otherwise.

If you want to see how skillfully this technique can be used, watch for Christian artists in your area who offer free shows. These are usually done in churches and not promoted to the general public, so if you're not affiliated with a church, you may have to find somebody who is in order to find out about them.

From my experience, Christian artists are the most skilled at making money this way. Part of this is because of the "ministry" aspect of Christian music; people want to support evangelism. Beyond that, though, the lack of Christian music venues, outside churches, has created a culture in which musicians in this genre have had to get very creative when it comes to being able to make money and get gigs.

Even if you're not a Christian performer, the technique of playing a free show and making money on the backend is still a powerful one. It has not only been used by musicians of all genres—it is also commonly used by both street performers and comedians. Keep an eye out for people doing shows in this way.

WAYS TO SELL MERCHANDISE AT YOUR LIVE SHOW

Even with newer options in music distribution, such as online and digital options, the majority of independent musicians sell the bulk of their products via the very old-school method of a "merch table" at live events. Here is how to sell even more:

Announce It – If you don't tell people you have something for sale, they won't know.

"The song is called <<SONG NAME>>. It's on our new album, <<ALBUM NAME>>, which is available in the back at the merch table."

When you say this, hold up the album in one hand and point to the merch table with your other hand!

If you want to really drive things home, let people know how much it is and what a bargain they're getting ...

"The song is called <<SONG NAME>>. It's on our new album, <<ALBUM NAME>>, which is available for only <<PRICE>> in the back at the merch table. For the same cost as a cup of coffee at Starbucks, you'll get 10 of the songs you've heard tonight to play over and over again."

Nervous about really going for the jugular with your sales pitch? Have fun with it!

"The song is called <<SONG NAME>>. It's on our new album, <<ALBUM NAME>>, which is available for only <<PRICE>> in the back at the merch table. For the same cost as a cup of coffee at Starbucks, you'll get 10 of the songs you've heard tonight to play over and over again. Plus, everybody who buys this album tonight will walk away with 10 times the sex appeal they had when they came in, and how much is that worth?"

Don't assume people know anything—the name of the song, the album it's on, or where in the room to get the album. Your audience isn't stupid, but they're busy and they have other things on their minds. It takes a few attempts before most people pay attention. Also, people are coming in and out of your show all the time, so they're not hearing your message nearly as much as you think they are.

Think of your onstage announcements similar to a radio host announcing the name of the station you're listening to. During a one-hour timeslot, the station will "ID" itself (or the show being aired) several times. If you have fun with it, like the example above, people will enjoy that part of your show as much as the music.

Get People Involved – People don't come to a show just to watch it; they want to be part of it.

If you see a woman in the front row, singing her ass off, get her on stage to help sing background vocals on a song. Or just acknowledge her.

Something like this is the perfect opportunity to hand out a CD or T-shirt. It not only activates the law of reciprocity with the fan you acknowledge, but it also sends a message to the audience that you reward people for participating in the show—while letting them know you have merchandise available.

Bring It To Them – When you're doing a good job of keeping fans engaged, they're not going to get up and buy your stuff. You could wait until the end of your performance, which is an option, but after your performance, there may be another band after you, people may be ready to go home, or people may be out of money. If you wait until after the show, you'll miss out on the valuable "social proof" of having people in the crowd with your shirts or music.

The solution to this is to bring your offer to people. More or less, this is an upscale version of that guy in the baseball stands yelling, "Ice cold beer here!"

NOTE: I understand that the following paragraphs contain information that won't work for everybody and will be offensive to some. Even if you don't feel comfortable using the following script or setting up a related scenario, don't neglect learning about the psychology behind why this works.

To bring your music or merch directly to your audience, you'll need somebody who is attractive for this job. Everyone knows that beautiful people have significant advantages in human society. One of those advantages is that people are more likely to talk to them (and buy what they're selling), especially in a sexually charged environment like a bar or club, which is where most music acts play.

If you don't have a connection with somebody who can get results, such as an attractive friend or fan, you can hire somebody via a modeling agency. Doing so can be done at a reasonable price.

Make sure you tell your attractive "sales agent" that the most important part of the interaction, probably more important than a one-time sale, is that they get the person's contact information, so you'll be able to keep in touch with him/her and get them to come to other shows (and otherwise spend more money with you) in the future.

Suggest starting the conversation by asking for a name and email address.

Example:

"What's your name?"

When you get it, respond:

"Hi, <<HIS NAME>>. I'm <<SALES AGENT NAME>> and I work with <<BAND NAME>>. Are you having a good time tonight?"

Wait for the person to say yes. Then ask one of the following questions:

IF THE PERSON IS WITH A DATE, SAY... *"<<HIS NAME>>. You two look great tonight. Would you mind if I take your photo for <<NAME OF POPULAR SOCIAL MEDIA SITE>>?"*

IF THE PERSON APPEARS TO BE SINGLE, SAY... "<<HIS NAME>>, *I'm taking photos for <<NAME OF POPULAR SOCIAL MEDIA SITE>>. Want to be in a picture with me?"*

Wait for a response. It will usually be yes.

"<<HIS NAME>>, we're taping the show tonight. Give me your email address and I'll send you the photo I just took and a link to download the recording."

(If you're not taping the show, you'll obviously want to modify this. But you really should be taping the show!)

At this point, get a name and email address.

"<<HIS NAME>>, thank you. I'll send everything to your email tomorrow, and you can write back and let me know what you think."

Then pause.

"<<HIS NAME>>, one more thing. <<BAND NAME>> is offering <<NEW CD>> for only $10 tonight. Plus, if you buy one right now, because I like you, I'll throw in a free T-shirt, just like the one I'm wearing. Sound good?"

Then pause. Most of the time, you'll get the sale. Here's why:

You've established the connection and built rapport through use of the person's name and by giving him something in return for an email address. People want to help their friends and "complete" any actions that social standards say require reciprocity. Additionally, you've gotten them comfortable agreeing with you and have built momentum for them to continue doing so by using the "yes ladder."

Even if you don't get the sale at this moment, because you're sending recordings of the show and photos, you've got a good reason to email to continue the conversation. Just because somebody says "no" right now doesn't mean you won't get a "yes" later.

Offer Combos – If you want a good example of how this technique is used, go to the "personal hygiene" aisle of your local mega-retailer. You'll see toothpaste tubes combined with a free toothbrush, mouthwash combined with a free "travel size" bottle, and more.

CDs and DVDs are cheap to produce, but can have a high perceived value, depending on what they contain. It's easy to build combos using CDs and DVDs—holiday-related combos, acoustic combos, etc.

Offer an Upsell – This is where you offer a customer who is already buying one of your more expensive items an upgrade or other add-on in an attempt to make a more profitable sale.

The most popular upsells happen at fast food restaurants ...

"Would you like fries with that?"

"Make it a combo?"

When selling a CD, a good upsell would be: *"Would you like a second copy of <<ALBUM NAME>> for $1 to give to a friend?"*

This $1 covers the cost of production and encourages word of mouth, but more importantly, it gets the buyer more invested in the purchase, since he now has a friend to share the experience with.

Single-Bill Prices – Isn't it annoying when you get behind somebody in the checkout line who wants to pay for something with exact change (or by writing a check) or with partial payments via multiple credit cards?

The quicker you are at taking money and getting people what they need, the more customers you'll be able to serve. One way to do this is by using "single-bill" prices. That means $1, $5, $10 or $20. If your CD is worth $7, either find a way to make a package worth $10 or drop the price to $5.

Use a "Merchandise Ladder" – Just like a ladder makes it easier to climb the side of a wall (letting you use small steps rather than one big leap), a "merchandise ladder" makes it easier for people to buy things from you.

As a musician, you're probably familiar with this concept, as it's often used in the marketing of musical instruments. For example, Fender has a "Squire" brand for people who want a low-priced, entry guitar. Under the Fender brand, they have a series of guitars made in Mexico, a series made in Japan, an "American Standard" series made in the USA, and "custom shop" options for those wanting a one-of-a-kind instrument.

A merchandise ladder gives people something to compare. Sometimes people "skip" rungs on the ladder.

Setting up your products in this way gives you something to sell to people on limited budgets, as well as a "better" option for people who prefer something of higher quality, more volume, or more prestige.

An example "merchandise ladder" for you to use:

Bumper Sticker – $1

Download Card – $5

CD – $10

Shirt – $10

DVD – $15

CD, Shirt, and DVD Combo – $20

The majority of acts don't sell as many DVDs as they do CDs, so a DVD, if sold by itself, may not be a good investment. When a DVD is packaged with a combo, though, such as the one above, the DVD may actually get people to buy your highest-priced item rather than nothing at all, simply because it adds perceived value to the package.

Make the "Irresistible Offer" – This is a good place to use a combo, although it's not a requirement. As long as you have something that's too good to pass up, even if it's one item, you can have an "irresistible offer."

There are two sides to every sale:

- **Cost** – This is what somebody gives in exchange for what you're offering. It can include money, but also time, commitment, risk of embarrassment, blood, sweat, or tears. It's what somebody has to trade in exchange for an opportunity, product, or service.

- **Value** – This is what somebody gets from you. It can be enjoyment, prestige, ease, or power.

A common thing people do when they're not getting the sales they want is to lower the selling price. This is a huge mistake.

Anything will sell if the price is low enough. You could sell music to a deaf Amish guy if you dropped the price enough. You won't be able to do it for long, though.

A much better option is to add value to your offer. What is something that a deaf Amish guy could use?

If you can come up with an answer for that question, you've got the skills necessary to develop an "irresistible offer" for your fans.

While this is an extremely effective approach for moving large numbers of albums and other merchandise, you'll want to be careful how often you use it. While you should be able to make a little profit on each item you sell, discounting prices too much may cause your audience to lower the perceived value of what you have, which is just the opposite of what you want.

Remember that the "irresistible offer" is the real goal of this. When you go for this option, it should create an "event" people feel won't happen again.

Example:

> *"Thanks for coming tonight! This is my first time in Chunky, Mississippi. I'm playing here again on January 11th and I'd love to see you again. If you'll promise to tell a friend about the good time you've had tonight, I'll give you my new CD for only $1 and throw in a free ticket for the January 11th show, so we can hang out again."*

You'll break even on the CD, you'll get the fan used to spending money with you, and you'll facilitate a good recommendation. In addition, because almost nobody goes to see live music alone, anybody who gets one of your free tickets will likely bring others along, so you'll have a bigger crowd next time.

Make It Quick – You have only a limited amount of time when selling at a venue, so get people taken care of as quickly as possible.

Even though more and more people are using credit and debit cards to pay for things, most transactions at a live event are still cash. Use the "single bill" strategy mentioned earlier to speed things up when making change.

For fans who want to pay by credit or debit card, have a dedicated person to handle these transactions. Services like Square and PayPal will allow you to take credit card payments via mobile phones. Both services are scalable, and you can easily add additional card readers to speed up the transaction process even more as your sales volume grows. Visit SquareUp.com or PayPal.com for details.

If you take checks, don't bother with an ID. You'll get burned on occasion, but you'll more than make up for it in volume.

Be Organized – Again, speed is important. Looking at the tags of shirts, trying to find the right size, will hold up the line. To help you with this, sort T-shirts by both size and style before you start selling them. If you're selling combo packages, have them ready.

The Nuclear Option – This is a long-term strategy that works best when you're brand new to an area; have a big, one-time crowd that is more interested in the other act(s) playing (such as when you're opening for a major-label artist), or when you want to make a good impression on a club owner.

Make custom drink tickets.

Business cards can be used, as they're small, sturdy, and inexpensive. If you're worried about piracy, it's easy to stop by "validating" your tickets with an ink stamp. A self-inking date stamp, available from any office supply store, works just fine.

Before the show, make a deal with the bar or drink vendor. You should be able to work a deal for some discount drinks, since you're buying in bulk, but if not, pay retail, and figure out a way to make your numbers work without the discount.

One option that might get you a discount is to include a tip with every drink. For example, if a beer is $5, offer $4 plus an additional $1 tip for each ticket redeemed. It's still $5, but you'll have the service staff on your side, and that can help a lot when it comes to getting booked again and keeping your fans happy.

Note that you shouldn't have to buy anything ahead of time. At the end of the night, you'll simply pay for however many drink tickets have been redeemed.

On stage, use a variation of the following scripts to let fans know about the drink tickets:

> *"Thanks for coming tonight! You guys have been such a great crowd. I want to buy each of you a drink. During this next song, if you buy my new album for just $5, I'll buy you a beer. In five*

minutes, we're going to do a toast together, so hit the merch table and have a drink on me!"

Or:

"Thanks for coming tonight! You guys have been such a great crowd, I want to buy you a drink. During this next song, if you buy my new album for just $10, I'll throw in a free T-shirt and I'll buy you a beer, too. In five minutes, we're going to do a toast together, so hit the merch table and have a drink on me!"

You're in this to get fans, spread your music, and keep the club happy. This does all three.

You'll build rapport with fans by giving them a deal, a piece of the experience to take home with them, and personal interaction that they can't get elsewhere. You'll spread your music via the albums you sell and the word of mouth you help to create. You'll keep the venue happy by packing people in, giving them a good time, and selling lots of drinks.

WHAT TO DO WHEN PEOPLE SAY NO

Here are reasons people wouldn't buy an album at a live show and how you can work around these issues:

They're not carrying any money.

There are several solutions to this:

Let the person send you a check or email the money via a service such as PayPal.

You may not have 100 percent follow-through, but you'll have more people listening to your music (and hopefully sharing it with others). Don't think of it as a risk. Assuming the CDs you're selling cost $1 to produce and you sell them for $10, you'll break even with only 10 percent of people following through.

You always have the option of giving a free CD to the person who says he isn't carrying any money. The downside to this is that, generally, people who get something free are less likely to value it than those who pay money. With that said, though, if it only cost you $1 to produce a CD and if you get the sense that person is eager to tell everyone he knows about you and your music, why not?

They need money for something else.

Lots of people are on tight budgets and, because they weren't planning on buying any music, won't have the extra money needed for it. Others would rather spend the cash in their pockets on booze. Either way, "need money for something else" is something that will keep you from selling your CDs or merch.

When you get a response to your offer such as this, you have two options to move your music. Again, either let the person pay you by check or PayPal or give the person a CD for free.

In the case of paying later, say something such as:

> *"I understand. You know, it's more important that I get my music into the hands of a fan than try to make money right now. Why don't I just give you the CD tonight and you just send me the money when you can. No rush."*

When it comes to giving a CD, say something such as:

> *"I understand. You know, it's more important that I get my music into the hands of a fan than try to make money right now. Why don't I just give you the CD and, instead of paying for it, you tell five of your friends about us?"*

The goodwill you generate from either of these actions will be worth more than what you'd make from a CD.

They don't want to carry a CD around or prefer downloadable music.

If you don't have a bag on you, carrying around a CD all night can be a bitch. And more and more people are listening to music via mobile phone, MP3 players, and stereo equipment that won't play CDs. Both are legitimate excuses that you'll need to be able to work around.

You can sell a USB flash drive. Flash drives are cheap and getting cheaper every day. They're easy to carry around, plus, they have a use beyond just holding your music, so they're easy to sell.

You can also sell a "download card." This is a good way to satisfy the person who wants something physical to hold or collect, but not necessarily a CD.

Lots of companies can get you hooked up with download cards, but if you're already selling your music via CD Baby, the easiest way to add them to your product line is to purchase cards from their parent company, Disc Makers.

Here is what you'll get from them:

> *"Music Download Cards are full-color cards that feature your album artwork and a unique code that allows users to download your album at CD Baby. You decide how much to sell the cards for (or give them away for free if you want to), and your customers can download your music at their leisure."*

Download cards can sell well for several reasons:

- They're small and easy to carry (for both you and your fans).

- They deliver music in the way people want to consume it (downloads).

- They can be easily sold at a gig, unlike traditional downloads.

- They're inexpensive to manufacture and have a huge markup.

- They're collectible—you can change the art and sell the same "album" more than once.

In addition to all these things, they're great for encouraging your fans to tell their friends about you. If you decide to sell downloadable cards, I encourage you to give people two instead of one, and encourage them to give the extra to a friend. This will start the conversation about you and your music, which will hopefully result in the fan who purchased your music bringing somebody else along the next time you're in town.

Their friend bought the CD and will make copies.

Sure, it's technically illegal, but it happens. And why try to stop it? These people are providing you with free promotion that can be worth a lot more money than the cost of a lost CD sale.

- Make it easy to sign up for your mailing list. If somebody has hijacked your sale, you still have an opportunity for future sales. Encourage people to get on your mailing list, so you can keep in touch and let them know about other products and live performances.

- Sell a T-shirt. While you can, technically, copy a T-shirt, most people don't. This is the perfect example of something that is easier to buy than duplicate, so take advantage of it by focusing on T-shirt (and other merchandise) sales when playing areas such as college campuses, where copying music is more popular than buying it.

SELLING MUSIC BEYOND THE LIVE SHOW

Most acts aren't on tour constantly, so if you want to sell music outside of live performance situations, you need to have your music available in other ways that people like to buy music. That might sound obvious, and it should be obvious, but an unbelievably high percentage of musicians screw this up by trying to reinvent the business of music distribution or telling their fans how music should be both purchased and consumed.

Fans don't care about the "business" of the music industry. They don't care if you hate iTunes and would rather have your music available exclusively in small, indie record stores.

Fans want music in the way they want it. Period.

What does this mean to you?

It means, if you want to sell music, you need to have your music available where music is selling. Right now, the main place that is happening, like it or not, is via online retailers like iTunes and Amazon.

Small, indie record stores are great and provide an experience that you can't get from an online retailer, but most people don't care about "experience" enough to get in their cars, fight traffic, find a parking space, find your album, and fight traffic a second time to hand over their money for your music. You cannot rely on these stores alone.

If people don't like their options for purchasing your music, they'll do one of two things: steal your music or forget you and your music.

If you want to sell music, you have to make it easier to buy than steal. In addition, it has to be something people can do right now, before they forget and move on to other things in their lives.

How do you do that? Fortunately, it's extremely easy.

CD Baby is the largest online music distribution company for independent music. The company offers both physical and digital distribution, as well as warehousing and shipping of CDs, DVDs, and vinyl.

In short, CD Baby can get your music into digital retailers like iTunes and Amazon (and over a dozen others from around the world), as well as distribute physical product for you via postal mail. You'll deal with a single company and have your music available to 99 percent of online music buyers.

If you have an album and about $50, you can make your album available throughout the world via CD Baby and its partners.

Visit CDBaby.com for more info.

So what about the people who want a physical product and love the "record store" experience? They're certainly dwindling in numbers, but those who fall into this category are great people to have in your corner—they buy more music than the average person, they go to more live shows, and they're more likely to tell their friends about music they enjoy.

Unfortunately, the number of record stores for these people to shop in is getting smaller and smaller each year. However, there are still some great independent record stores in business, and if there is demand for your music in an area that has a store, by all means, have your music for sale there.

The Alliance of Independent Media Stores (AIMS) is a group made up of forward-thinking, locally owned music stores that are finding ways to compete in the changing record industry environment. Remember when record stores were cool? Hit a store that's a member of AIMS and you'll find they still are.

AIMS will work with you to help you sell more music. They offer audio and video listening station programs, online marketing support, and custom promotional opportunities to introduce your music to their customers.

All stores report to Soundscan, CMJ, and StreetPulse. Sales charts appear weekly in *CMJ New Music Report*, as well as being an element of the Billboard Tastemakers chart.

Visit TheAllianceRocks.com for more info.

Taking advantage of both options is your best bet for reaching the maximum number of people.

A third option to consider is going direct.

The one area in which I recommend most acts handle direct sales on their own is when transactions are done face to face, such as at the merchandise area of a live show. This will give you more control over pricing and package options, and also put you on the front line to personally see what people are buying, how much they're willing to pay, the questions they're asking about existing items, and requests for items you don't yet have available but would profit from if you did.

If you've got a website for your music, it's simple to sell music, both physical and digital, directly to your fans. Services such as Authorize. net, VeriSign, and PayPal will allow you to accept both credit cards and online checks, and delivering the purchase can be done via a "secret link" in an email or a CD sent via postal mail.

Listed below are some pros and cons of selling your music direct to fans:

Pros:

More Money – Fewer middlemen, like CD Baby and iTunes, means more money for you.

Quick Payment – Depending on your merchant services provider, you can be paid as quickly as that day.

Names and Addresses – When you sell directly to people, you'll have access to certain information that you won't get via a distributor, such as the names and addresses of your customers. This can be both helpful and valuable if you're tracking where albums are selling or have a mailing list.

Cons:

Customer Service – You're a musician, not tech support, the billing department, or the shipping department. You become these things when you sell your own music, though. Are you up for that?

Trust – People today trust buying things online more than ever, but there is still a lot of paranoia about giving credit card and other personal information online, especially to lesser-known sites. Some people won't order directly from you simply because they don't trust your site.

Accounting – You didn't become a musician to deal with inventory and tax records, but these are things you'll have to deal with when you sell direct to people.

The Time Suck – If you want to grow your music business, you should be spending your time doing things that nobody else can do. For more musicians, that means spending your time writing, recording, and performing music.

CD Baby will handle all your online orders, both digital and physical. It's trusted by consumers (and partners with other trusted companies, like Amazon and iTunes). It takes care of accounting and sends payments to you weekly, and at the end of the year, you'll know exactly how much money you made. CD Baby will handle the customer service issues of lost packages, disputed credit cards, and download problems.

With this option available for a modest price, when it comes to selling music online, why bother doing it yourself?

CATERING TO THE COLLECTORS

I don't know the specifics about how music will be delivered in the future. Nobody does. Based on what we've seen with other forms of entertainment and communication options, though, it will probably be some kind of subscription service that is bundled with a mobile device.

It will be "all you can eat" for a monthly fee, much like subscription television.

With that said, I also know that people like to collect things. Some of them like to collect music. This is a great opportunity for you to leverage the content you already have, whether it be specific songs or specific recordings of songs.

Here are five ways to do it:

Box Sets – Same stuff you've already released in a new wrapper and possibly bundled with something exclusive, such as a new song(s) or a live recording. This is like a "greatest hits" collection on steroids—more music and better packaging.

Signed – Same thing you've been selling elsewhere, but with your signature on it.

This is one a lot of acts have a hard time getting their heads around, and although it doesn't work for everybody, it will work in more situations than you might think. People want to feel connected to your music, and they want something that nobody else or very few people have. This is a good way to satisfy both of those things.

Colored Vinyl – The ultimate in hipster and "I have something nobody else has" satisfaction, putting your music on colored vinyl is a great way to get a premium price for it.

A great way for you to make this happen is to go to United Record Pressing in Nashville and get its "randomly mixed vinyl" option. It's cheaper than black, and every record will look different, with an individual pattern made up of the different colors of vinyl used.

Other vinyl options available from United include "split color" records, with your choice of two different solid or translucent colors.

No turntable? No problem! United offers you the option to allow anybody who purchases a vinyl record to get the same music via online downloads, which is a real selling point.

Special Packaging – This can be done with a standard album, but is best when the standard album is combined with a few bonus tracks. Both iTunes and Amazon are masters of this when it comes to downloadable albums, which proves the concept works with a nonphysical album. For most acts, though, it works even better when you give people a physical album they can hold.

I've found the best way to do this is to package your CD in a DVD case. It gives you more space for a cool cover as well as a larger booklet.

The downside of this is that some people will get confused and think they're buying a DVD. Because of this, an even better option is to package a DVD and CD together. For example, a CD of your new album with bonus tracks along with a DVD of "behind the scenes" videos from when you were in the studio, rehearsals, or life on the road.

Limited Edition – This is more of a technique to increase sales rather than something to sell. To create a "limited-edition" product, simply take any of the options listed above and limit the availability. For added effect, hand-number each item.

For example, if you're going to limit the number of items to 100, you'd number each 1/100, 2/100, 3/100, and so on. For many fans, lower numbers are worth more.

Limited-edition albums are the perfect format for print-on-demand and short-run CDs, as well as download cards, because runs of 100 or less are relatively cheap. In addition, limited-edition, event-specific T-shirts almost always sell well.

THINK BEYOND MUSIC

Remember my friend who owns the gas station that was mentioned earlier in the book?

"I don't make a lot of money on gas. It's very expensive. My money is made on auto service, beer, cigarettes, and candy," he told me.

Music may be the same way for you. Don't get caught up thinking just because you're marketing yourself as a "musician" that you have to make the majority of your income from music.

Right now, the following acts are selling more T-shirts and other merchandise than they are music. These items are what keep the music alive, so don't neglect them.

- The Ramones

- The Grateful Dead

- 2Pac

- Sex Pistols

- Led Zeppelin

- Motorhead

- The Doors

Even if you are selling lots of music, if you're not selling non-music merchandise, you're leaving money on the table. You're also missing out on great advertising.

You don't have to go as far as Gene Simmons of KISS does and license your name to create a line of caskets, cremation urns, prayer cards, registry books, and candles. However, while keeping things within reason, "If it will sell, you should sell it" is a good rule of thumb.

To start, keep things simple with the "basics" of T-shirts and stickers. If you're looking to go beyond this, posters, patches, guitar picks, beanies, buttons, key chains, hoodies, and baseball caps work well for many acts.

Unsure of whether an item will sell? Thanks to digital printing, it's very easy to do a short run of just about any clothing or print item. You won't get the break on price that you will with traditional manufacturing, but it may be worth your time and expense to do a limited test campaign, since you don't want to be stuck with hundreds (or thousands) of an item you're unable to sell.

The music and other merchandise you sell at shows (and elsewhere) is more than just a way for you to make extra money. These items allow your fans to take the live show experience home with them, share what you do with their friends, and feel more connected to you.

You didn't get into this business because you wanted to be in sales, but like it or not, selling music and other merchandise is what makes the difference between an average career and an extraordinary one. A well-organized merchandising plan can turn losing gigs into profitable ones, keep you on the road, and keep your bank account flush with money.

Will You Do Me a Favor?

I wrote this book to help musicians. The more people who know about it (and your good experience with it), the more people I can help.

If you *like* this book, please do me a favor and ...

- **Tell People** - Tell your musician friends, post a link to MusicMarketing.com on your site or via social media, and buy copies for the people in your band.
- **Leave a Review on Amazon** - Visit Amazon.com (or wherever you buy books) and post a review letting people know why you think this book is helpful for musicians.

If you *want to improve* this book, please do me a favor and ...

- **Tell Me** - Send me a message on Twitter (@davidhooper) and let me know what you didn't like as well as suggestions for improving the next edition.

If you *think this book sucks*, please do me a favor and ...

- **Let Me Buy Back Your Copy** – If you're not completely satisfied with this book, send it back to me along with your receipt and I'll gladly write you a check for the full purchase price.

Contact Me

Have music marketing questions? I'm happy to help you!

The best way to get in touch with me is via Twitter. @davidhooper is my username.

Facebook.com/MusicMarketing is my Facebook page.

MusicMarketing.com is my website. Visit for free bonus materials to help you.